The
Shroud
of Turin

The most up-to-date analysis of all the facts
regarding the Church's controversial relic.

The Shroud of Turin

C. BERNARD RUFFIN

2122332

Our Sunday Visitor Publishing Division
Our Sunday Visitor, Inc.
Huntington, Indiana 46750

ISBN: 0-87973-617-8
LCCCN: 99-70509

Medical illustrations by Marie T. Dauenheimer
Cover design by Rebecca Heaston
Cover art courtesy of the Holy Shroud Guild

PRINTED IN THE UNITED STATES OF AMERICA

617

Contents

Acknowledgments

This book could never have come into being without the gracious assistance of many individuals who gave me their time and resources.

William Accousti, who provided help on Internet materials and lent me books from his library.

Alan D. Adler, who answered questions and provided assistance in two very long telephone conversations and also read and corrected those portions of my manuscript that dealt with his research.

Robert Bucklin, forensic pathologist, who provided me with a copy of his latest paper, as well as advice.

Marie T. Dauenheimer, a board-certified medical illustrator, who provided the sketches for this book. She and her husband, Dr. Samuel Strong Dunlap, a physical anthropologist, answered many of my questions, provided me with encouragement, and read and commented on my manuscript.

John P. Jackson, who with his wife, Rebecca, heads the Turin Shroud Center of Colorado, answered a number of my questions in a telephone conversation.

Moe Lerner, a physician with many years of experience in emergency rooms, who answered many of my questions about the injuries suffered by the man of the Shroud.

Father Joseph Marino, O.S.B., of St. Louis Abbey, St. Louis, Missouri, who provided me with a useful bibliography of Shroud materials.

The late Father Adam J. Otterbein, C.S.S.R., of the Holy Shroud Guild, with whom I corresponded.

Isabel H. Piczek, of the Construction Art Center of Los Angeles, who answered my letters and provided copies of some of her papers.

The late Father Peter M. Rinaldi, S.D.B., whom I visited twice at his office at the Corpus Christi Church of Port Chester, New York, and who encouraged me to write about the Shroud and put me in touch with others who could help me.

I also wish to thank the Holy Shroud Guild for photographic materials and permission to use them.

The Shroud (shown displayed vertically) at the 1973 exposition.

Introduction

The "Holy Shroud," also known as the "Shroud of Turin," or simply, the "Shroud," an ancient cloth which bears the clear and unmistakable imprint of a human body, identified by many as that of the founder of Christianity, has been the subject of dozens of scientific tests, scores of books, and hundreds of articles in the last half of the twentieth century. I am neither artist, art historian, anthropologist, chemist, nor physicist. As a historian, in this book I do not pretend to break new ground or claim novel insights, but rather set forth in a clear and plain way for the general reader the historical and scientific facts that have made this aged linen the subject of the most intense interest throughout the centuries, and, in particular, the last hundred years. My aim, therefore, is to describe: (1) the physical appearance of the Shroud; (2) why it has been of interest to the theological and scientific communities; (3) what is known of its history; (4) what studies have been done upon it; and (5) what theories and hypotheses have been proposed as to its nature and origin.

**A modern icon of Christ based on the Shroud of Turin,
painted by Agemian.**

Chapter 1

'So Incomparable a Portrait'

The "Holy Shroud" is a large, oblong linen cloth, of great but contested age, which is normally housed in a chapel built especially for it in the Cathedral of Saint John the Baptist in the city of Turin, in northern Italy. It is displayed only on rare occasions, contained in a frame that shows the length of the cloth parallel to the ground.

The cloth, marked by various blemishes and stains, measures fourteen feet three inches long and three feet seven inches wide — or, according to the measurement in use in the Middle East in the first century, eight cubits by two.[1] Experts in the field of textiles have determined that the threads were hand-spun and the fabric hand-woven in what is known as a "three-to-one herringbone twill." This was a type of weaving practiced in the Middle East at least as far back as two thousand years ago.[2]

The linen has a number of scratches and burn holes, as well as water stains. The features most visible to the naked eye are two dark blemishes, one on each side of the fainter body image, running parallel to the sides of the cloth. Along these streaks, on both front and back images, on either side of the shoulders and on either side of the knee, are diamond-shaped patches. These are the result of a fire that broke out in December 1532, in the chapel in France where it was housed. The patches cover holes that were burned through the folded cloth by hot metal.

There some other burn marks on the fabric which are much less obvious. There is a row of three small holes with burnt edges on either side of the crossed hands on the frontal view, and similar configurations on each side of the posterior portions of the figure on the back image. No one knows the cause of this damage, which seems to have been the result of a hot poker being thrust three times through the center of the cloth. Because these holes are evident in a copy of the Shroud which dates to 1516, it is clear that they predated the damage from the fire.

A second fire, during the night of April 11-12, 1997, once again menaced the Shroud, but through the courageous actions of the firefighters from Turin's Twenty-First Brigade, who smashed the display case to rescue the celebrated artifact, a conflagration that heavily damaged the Cathedral and the adjoining Royal Chapel left the Shroud untouched.

Less evident on the Shroud than the sixteenth-century fire damage are the two faint head-to-head straw-colored images of an undressed man that appear in the center of the cloth, one of the front of the body, the other of the back, with the feet of both images facing the outer margins of the fabric. There are only a few inches between the front and back images of the head. It seems as though a body had been laid on its back at one end of the cloth, which was then drawn over the front of the man, and that somehow an image was made of him.

If the viewer approaches too close, he (or she) is unable to see anything except stains. Standing three to six feet away from the cloth, he will be able to discern some detail. From the frontal image the observer will be able to make out the shape of a man with long hair and a beard, with his hands folded over his pelvic area and his knees slightly drawn up. Around the head, wrists, and feet are what appear to be bloodstains, especially on the back image. Viewing the cloth with the naked eye, it is hard to make out anything else — much less determine — whether the image is a painting. With its ghostly face and great owl-like eyes, it certainly does not look much like a real image of a real person.

In fact, in the late nineteenth century, this image was considered by many simply as an interesting work of art. Then, on May 28, 1898, the Shroud was photographed for the first time, with amazing results. When photographer Secondo Pia viewed the negative of the Shroud in his darkroom, he was astounded because he seemed to be looking at a real photograph of a real human body. Peter Rinaldi, a priest born in Turin who devoted his long life to the study of the Shroud, wrote, "A positive picture appeared on the negative plate. Normally, when a person or object is photographed, a negative image is produced on the negative film or plate, because the lights and shades of the person or object are registered by lights, and lights by darks. . . . In the case of the Shroud, the figures that had been photographed . . . were already negatives [and] . . . the lights and shades of the images on the Shroud were already reversed. Being reinverted on the negative plate, they appeared there positive."[3] It was therefore only when the first *negative* images were made of the Shroud that striking anatomical details could be for the first time observed.

Rinaldi noted that the face of the *positive* image — that is, the one that can be seen with the eye — looks like a mask, but when shown in negative it "takes on a wondrous expression . . . an expression which has elicited the admiration of countless artists."[4] The man of the Shroud has a long, somewhat narrow face and a long nose of the type stereotypically associated with Jews. He has a moustache and beard, somewhat disheveled. The eyes are closed. The man has evidently suffered extensive injuries. His hair, which frames the face, is matted with what appears to be blood and there are several trickles extending from the scalp, one as far as the eyebrow. The image of the back of the head reveals that the man evidently wore his hair drawn back in a long queue. Apparent bloodstains are evident there, too. One cheek and the bridge of the nose appear swollen. Nevertheless, the man wears an expression of majestic serenity.

The man's body is covered with marks — more than one hundred of them — that are consistent with the wounds left by the Roman *flagrum,* a short, double-thonged, bone-tipped whip commonly used to flog prisoners. Medical and forensic experts have noted that these wounds, especially evident on the dorsal, or back image, are in the shape of double knobs.

In the region of one of the shoulder blades is evidence of a wound caused by a heavy object that rubbed off the skin there, as if, perhaps, the man, shortly before death, had balanced a heavy beam on the shoulder. The hands are crossed over the pelvic area. There is a large bloodstain on the left wrist. The right wrist is hidden beneath the left, but a trickle of blood that runs along the right forearm suggests an origin in a similar wound in the left wrist. Flows of blood on the forearms have suggested to many who have studied the cloth that the man's arms had been extended as if in crucifixion, just before death.

Wounds on the feet are visible in the back imprint, and on the right side of the chest there is a large, open wound, which poured forth an abundant flow of blood and serum that can be seen even in the image of the back — a fact which suggests that blood flowed from the side and trickled around the trunk of the body as it lay flat, making its way onto the back.[5]

When photographed and viewed as a negative, the Shroud of Turin reveals a remarkably detailed picture of an anatomically correct man who had been brutally whipped, who had carried something heavy on one shoulder, and who had been wounded in the head, hands, feet, and side. Art experts have been able to detect no evidence of brush strokes and have determined that, unlike the case of nearly all paintings, the coloring is spread in a non-directional way.

The images are of two types: the body image and the apparent bloodstains. Scientists who have studied the Shroud — with one notable and vocal exception — are convinced that the body image was created by some sort of dehydration process and that the bloodstains were caused by real blood. They also found that the body image is indelible, as more than two dozen types of laboratory solvents have been applied, at one time, to threads culled from the Shroud, to alter or remove the stain, but with no success.[6] Moreover, computer analysis has determined that the image is three-dimensional, which is a characteristic the Shroud does not share with normal paintings or even photographs. An art expert named C.D. Viale wrote, "In all my years of experience with pictorial productions, I have yet to see anything that approximates the image on the Shroud. That so incomparable a portrait of Christ, with no visible trace of paint, should be found *in reverse* on an ancient cloth is an enigma to which we art experts do not have a solution."[7]

We are now going to take a closer look at what physicians and forensic experts can tell us specifically about the physical condition of the man on the Shroud.

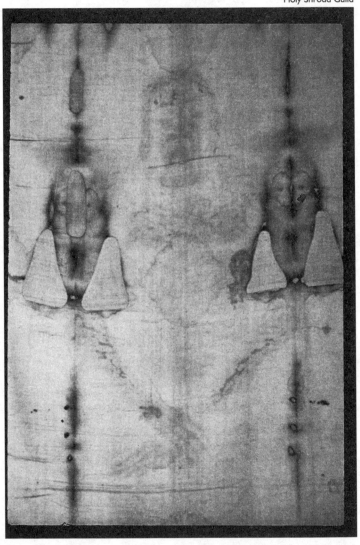

Closeup of the frontal image (1973 photo).

Chapter 11

The Shroud and the Pathologists

The Shroud has been studied over the years by many people with a medical background, several of whom published their findings. Three of those who wrote most extensively of their studies of the Shroud from a medical and pathological point of view were Pierre Barbet, Robert Bucklin, and Frederick Zugibe. The earliest was Barbet, who served as a battlefield surgeon during World War I and later headed the department of surgery at St. Joseph's Hospital in Paris. In 1950 he published a long study known in its English translation as *A Doctor at Calvary*. Dr. Robert van Zandt Bucklin, a forensic pathologist who served as deputy medical examiner for Los Angeles County, California, performed autopsies on over twenty-five thousand bodies. He authored at least seven articles about the Shroud from the point of view of his profession, published between 1958 and 1997. Dr. Frederick T. Zugibe, another forensic pathologist who held the position of chief medical examiner for Rockland County, New York, and taught at Columbia University's College of Physicians and Surgeons, wrote a book in 1981 entitled *The Cross and the Shroud.*

Even those who have studied the Shroud superficially agree that the image on it, whether the impress of a real body or not, is of a victim of crucifixion. This form of execution, which the Roman writer Cicero called "the most cruel and atrocious of punishments,"[8] was a common method of dispatching prisoners between approximately 200 B.C. and A.D. 400. Apparently it was first used by the Persians, who tied or impaled their victims on trees or upright posts.[9] Alexander the Great, the Macedonian king whose domain extended over the eastern Mediterranean area and the Middle East in the fourth century B.C., learned it from the Persians, and the Romans evidently picked up the practice from the Carthaginians,[10] whose empire was centered in what is now Tunisia. They seemed to have perfected it as the best way to carry out a sentence of death with the infliction of the greatest amount of suffering possible.

The Romans had innumerable ways of torturing people to death. A Roman citizen condemned to death had the privilege of a speedy and relatively painless death from decapitation. (St. Paul, for example, was a Roman citizen and was put to death in this way.) However, most people who lived in the Roman Empire — which for centuries embraced most of western Europe, all the regions around the Mediterranean Sea, and the Middle East, and was home (it has been estimated) to between thirty and one hundred million at a time — were not Roman citizens. If found guilty of a capital crime, they could count on a torturous and agonizing death through one of the many forms of execution in use. Nearly everyone knows of the practice of exposing the condemned in the arena to lions, leopards, bulls, panthers, and other wild beasts. In addition, Romans frequently burned their victims alive. Sometimes prisoners were locked in a metal chair which was heated by a fire beneath it until it was red hot and the victim slowly roasted. Torturers often raked all the flesh from the bones with iron claws. Sometimes they pulled the trunks of two saplings together, and fastened one leg of a condemned person on one trunk and the other leg on the other, and then cut the two saplings loose, so that the victim would be ripped in two pieces by the force of the boughs snapping back to their original position. But as a means of inflicting severe and prolonged torture, the Romans determined that there was nothing like crucifixion.

This punishment was especially popular with Roman authorities in what is now Israel, where during the time of Jesus there was strong desire for independence and an equally strong contempt for Roman rule that led to many rebellions, great and small. A generation after the time of Christ, subsequent to a serious revolt, Roman authorities crucified more than five hundred Jews a day in the environs of Jerusalem.[11]

From historical writing and archaeological evidence, there were several ways in which crucifixion was carried out. Prior to being fixed to the cross the condemned man (or woman) was often flogged, but usually not so severely as to weaken the prisoner so much that he was in danger of dying. Forced to walk to the place of execution, often with a placard around his neck describing his crime, the victim was sometimes made to carry part of the instrument upon which he was to meet his demise. The cross was usually in two parts. The *stipes,* which was an upright beam (often a tree trunk), was fixed permanently in the ground. The crossbeam, or *patibulum*, which archaeologists guess weighed between seventy-five and one hundred twenty-five pounds,[12] was carried on the shoulder of the prisoner. There has been considerable discussion among historians and archaeologists as to what happened next and how the prisoner was placed on the cross. The general consensus seems to be that after the prisoner's hands were fixed to the crossbeam, he was forced to rise or was lifted up and then backed up or hoisted onto the upright beam, to which the crossbeam was now nailed. At this point, the condemned man's feet were nailed to the front of the *stipes.* The wooden foot-rests seen on many crucifixes were apparently seldom used.[13]

Over the years the tradition developed that Jesus was the only person to be nailed to the cross. Many crucifixion scenes show the criminals put to death on either side of Christ on Calvary tied by ropes to the cross. Since the bodies of most of the victims of crucifixion were thrown into pits or left out to be eaten by animals, the remains of nearly all of the people so tortured have not survived. There does exist one skeleton, uncovered in a tomb in Jerusalem, dating from the approximate time of Christ, that shows signs of crucifixion. The man, whose name was evidently Jehohanan ben Hagwl, had been nailed through the feet, and his legs had been broken. A nail scratch on the bone of the right forearm suggested to several archaeologists that he had been nailed through the wrist. Some historians believe that nails and ropes were sometimes used together. At least one scholar was convinced that, for some reason, during the first century there was a trend away from the use of nails and towards the use of ropes.[14] At the time of Jesus, however, crucifixion with nails seems to have been typical in the Middle East.

There is a good deal of controversy as to how a victim of crucifixion died. Many historians believe that the victim of crucifixion, often stripped naked, was usually fixed to the cross in such a way that he was subject to increasingly severe muscle spasms, which progressively restricted his breathing until he suffocated. The only way a crucified man could avoid asphyxiation would be to raise himself by placing the weight of his body on the nails driven through his feet. When that agony became too great, he would sag down until the cramps forced him onto the nails in his feet again. This could go on for hours. In order to prolong the suffering of their victim, the executioners often attached an arm of wood to the upright, so that the condemned could rest and catch his breath by sitting on it. They often gave the prisoner something to drink, so that he would not die prematurely of dehydration. In this way, Roman executioners, if they so chose, could extend the torture of the condemned for several days. Then, when the executioners wanted to dispatch their victim, they took a mallet and broke the legs. In that way the prisoner could no longer raise his body and would slowly but surely suffocate. Some medical experts, on the other hand, believe that it was likely that most crucifixion victims died, not of asphyxiation, but rather of shock.

Pierre Barbet and others were convinced that before handing the body to family and friends or disposing of it, the executioners routinely made sure that the victim was really dead by stabbing him in the heart. Barbet quoted the third-century Roman writer Sextus Empiricus, who wrote, "The wound in the heart is the cause of death."[15] Archaeologist William Meacham disagreed, because Christian authors from the second and third century — a time when crucifixion was still common — wrote as if they believed that the issue of water and blood from the side was miraculous. He cited the third-century Christian writer Origen, who, in his defense of his faith against a Roman philosopher, pointed out that "in other dead bodies the blood congeals, and pure water does not flow forth; but the miraculous feature in the case of the dead body of Jesus was, that . . . blood and water flowed forth from the side."[16] Meacham pointed out that the flow of "water" and blood from the side is common in victims wounded in similar fashion to the man of the Shroud. The fact that Origen — who lived when crucifixions were common — treated this phenomenon as unusual convinced Meacham that the stabbing of crucifixion victims in the side was "a very rare happening."[17]

Crucifixion fell out of use among Christians during the early Middle Ages, probably because of its association with Jesus. Emperor Constantine I (c. 272-337), whose Edict of Milan legalized the practice of Christianity and who himself was baptized on his deathbed, forbade the imposition of crucifixion by "public tribunals." Crucifixions nevertheless were still carried out by "private tribunals" for a few years and were still permitted in the Eastern Roman Empire even later.[18] There is some evidence that crucifixion was widely used in the seventh century by Moslems to dispatch Christian prisoners. However, long before the thirteenth or fourteenth century — the time when some scholars claim the cloth and its image were fabricated — the practice of crucifixion had virtually, if not entirely, died out through the Mediterranean world. It seems, in fact, to have been completely unknown as a means of capital punishment in medieval Europe.

Because of the position of the body on the Shroud, one cannot simply take a tape measure to determine the height of the man represented on it. There have been various estimates of the height, ranging from five feet three-and-one-half inches, calculated by Vatican archivist Giuilio Ricci, to six feet six inches or more, by

Lynn Pincknett, editor of the *Macmillan Encyclopedia of the Paranormal*. Most of those who have studied the Shroud are convinced, however, that the man of the Shroud was no shorter than five feet eleven inches and no taller than six feet two inches.

Some would argue that the six-foot height of the man of the Shroud argues against its authenticity. There is, however, little concrete evidence to confirm the modern stereotype of the short stature of ancient people. We know the actual heights of almost no one in antiquity. The Roman historian Suetonius, in his *Lives of the Twelve Caesars*, gives detailed descriptions of the physical appearance of the first Roman emperors, and, without fail, indicates whether they were tall, short, or of medium height. In only one instance, however, does he give a precise figure, and that is in the case of Caesar Augustus, who stood just under five feet seven inches and was considered "short."[19] Greeks and Romans usually cremated their dead, so there is little skeletal evidence on which to draw any meaningful conclusions concerning the average height of people at the time of Christ. Although Jews did bury their dead, few skeletons from ancient times have been recovered intact. Apparently the most extensive collection was excavated from a burial cave in Jerusalem at a place called Giv'at-Mivtar. Archaeologists were able to harvest thirty-five well-preserved skeletons, eight of which are of adult males. The shortest of these men was about five feet two inches tall and the tallest was five feet eleven inches. The average height of the eight male skeletons was about five feet six inches.[20] If these few men were representative of their time and place, the man of the Shroud would have been about six inches taller than the average man (as a man six feet three or four inches would be today in America and Western Europe) — but there would have been nothing abnormal or anomalous about his height.

Actually, the posterior image is two-and-one-half inches longer than the frontal image. This seems to be a result of the way the cloth was folded over the corpse. The toes of the subject are not evident on the frontal image, but the soles of the feet appear on the dorsal image, suggesting that when the dead man was placed on his back on the Shroud and the long cloth was pulled over the face and trunk and legs, it proved a little too short to cover the toes.

Rodney Hoare (1927-1997), chairman for many years of the British Society for the Turin Shroud, insisted that the man of the Shroud was actually alive when the image was formed. In his 1994 book *The Turin Shroud is Genuine,* he described how he showed large prints of the Shroud, both in positive and negative, to Norman Lee, director of the East Midland Forensic Science Laboratory in England. After looking at the prints Lee was convinced that the side wound was superficial. He told Hoare, "That would have done little damage. Put your hand where the point entered as on the Shroud photograph, and then lift your arms to the side in the crucifixion position, and it was too high to damage anything if the wound came from below. It would have bled . . . and it might have allowed water between the lung and its cavity to come out at the same time. That water, the pleural effusion, would have been formed when the body was scourged. The lung would have been forced back, but even if the weapon had entered the lungs they can localise the injury."[21] Lee and his assistants believed that the man in the Shroud was merely in a coma when he was taken down from the cross and put in the tomb. Hoare, who was certain that the man was Jesus, speculated that the tomb was found empty because its occupant had revived, and that the resurrection appearances to the disciples were visits by a man who simply had never been dead!

There are several logical problems with this. Although Hoare points out that until fairly recent times it was common for comatose people to be buried alive, the fact remains that the men who ruled Jerusalem wanted Jesus dead, and if by some strange chance He had actually survived His attempted execution and had walked (or been helped) away from His intended tomb to make periodic visits to His followers (even if from a hiding place), they would have hunted Him down and made sure that He was permanently dead. Moreover, the wounds to the feet inflicted in crucifixion were such that, even if He had survived the cross, it is inconceivable that he could have been *walking* anywhere within three days of His ordeal, as we shall shortly see. It is also impossible to imagine Jesus' followers giving up their livelihoods and endangering their lives to travel all around the Roman Empire proclaiming eternal salvation through the resurrection of a man they knew to be a fraud!

Michael M. Baden, who served as deputy chief medical examiner of New York City for Queens County and afterwards worked as co-director of the Forensic Sciences Unit of the New York State Police, in 1980 examined a set of full-color photographs of the Shroud provided by *National Geographic Magazine,* as well as a set of black and white prints from the Holy Shroud Guild. He commented, "If I had to go into a courtroom, I could not say . . . whether the man was alive or dead."[22]

Virtually every medical expert other than Lee and Baden who has studied the Shroud is convinced that it shows the image of a man who is dead. J. Malcolm Cameron, a pathologist at London Hospital who studied color photographs of the Shroud, wrote in 1978, "the image of the face is indicative of one who . . . is not alive, for the linen cloth would act like a plastic membrane and would be sucked into the mouth and nostrils were the victim alive, as happens in tragic cases when a plastic bag is placed over the head of a child."[23] Moreover, some researchers have found further proof that the victim was dead in the appearance of the wound in the side. The stain showed that "the denser part of the blood" flowed first, followed by clear serum. This phenomenon "could not have taken place in the living body."[24] In addition, Frederick Zugibe reasoned, had the victim been alive, the Shroud would have been saturated with blood, because "even tiny wounds bleed profusely when the heart is beating."[25]

Although Baden insisted that he could not tell from his examination of the Shroud photographs whether rigor mortis was present, other medical experts who had looked at the image were able to discern this stiffening of the limbs which is a result of postmortem chemical changes. Zugibe dismissed as a "ridiculous concept" the idea that the man of the Shroud was still alive when he was wrapped in the cloth.[26] The body represented on the Shroud, he contended, shows "incontrovertible evidence of rigor mortis" in the position of the head and neck. The man of the Shroud appears, in fact, to have no neck, and this, the pathologist explained, is the case because when the victim died, the head fell forward and was quickly fixed in that position by the rigor mortis that occurs almost immediately after death in some cases of violent trauma, a phenomenon he observed many times in his practice as a medical examiner.[27]

Bucklin, slightly more cautious, observed that "the body appears to be in a state of rigor mortis, which is evidenced by an overall stiffness as well as specific alterations in the appearance of the lower extremities" as seen in the dorsal, or back, image. For example, "The imprint of the right calf is much more distinct than that of the left, indicating that at the time of death the left leg was rotated in such a way that the sole of the left foot rested on the ventral [lower] surface of the right foot with resultant slight flexion of the left knee," a position that was "maintained after rigor mortis developed."[28]

Malcolm Cameron agreed with Zugibe and Bucklin that "the position of the body as depicted on the Shroud is consistent with that of a crucified body in a state of post-mortem rigor."[29]

Not only were these pathologists satisfied that the man of the Shroud was in fact dead when laid out in the cloth, they also found extensive evidence of the trauma he suffered in the closing hours of his life. On the chest in the front image and on the length of the back image, from the shoulders, down the back, and covering the buttocks and legs, are dozens of little dumbbell-shaped wounds. Those familiar with Roman torture have noted their correspondence to the wounds inflicted by the Roman *flagrum*.

Baden, citing his experience that even badly damaged bodies that he examined in his morgue did not stain the shrouds in which they were wrapped, denied that the marks of a scourging would have left an imprint on the Shroud.[30] Other scholars were not of this opinion. Giulio Ricci, Vatican archivist, in his article "Historical, Medical, and Physical Study of the Holy Shroud" stated his conviction that the "Shroud Man" does in fact show signs of scourging. He described the instrument known as the "horrible scourge," which was banned from use on Roman citizens: "The blunt parts, consisting of pointed little metal [balls] or animal bones, placed two by two along the line of the three strips of leather or cord." Ricci also noted "two precise semicircles of blows, converging at two focal points."[31] This convinced him that the victim was scourged by two men. The only part of the body untouched was the area around the heart. Ricci speculated that the torturers deliberately avoiding striking the prisoner in a vital area because they would have been subject to severe punishment if they hastened the death of a man condemned to prolonged suffering.[32]

Ricci counted over two hundred twenty lashes.[33] While the Jews traditionally limited the strokes in a flogging to thirty-nine, the Romans usually imposed no limit. However, Ricci believed that the Roman practice was to limit the stripes inflicted on prisoners condemned to death so that they would not die prematurely. On the other hand, prisoners whose release was expected were frequently beaten to within an inch of their lives.[34]

The man was evidently stripped naked and whipped while bound to a post, with his hands over his head. Barbet wrote: "At first the strokes leave long vivid marks, long blue bruises beneath the skin. . . . Further marks are made by the balls of lead. Then the skin, into which the blood has crept, becomes tender and breaks under fresh blows. The blood pours out, shreds of skin become detached and hang down. The whole of the back is now no more than a red surface, on which great furrows stand out like marble; and here and there, everywhere, there are deeper wounds caused by the balls of lead."[35] In other words, the back of the man of the Shroud was torn to shreds.

Zugibe similarly observed that the bone (or metal) tip of the *flagrum* ripped small blood vessels, nerves, muscles, and skin. Because the marks are directed downward and inward from the center of the body, Zugibe was, like Ricci, convinced that the victim was flogged either by two men — or, perhaps, by a single soldier who periodically moved from one side of the man he was torturing to the other. On the basis of the injuries evident on the Shroud, Zugibe imagined that the victim must have "writhed, rolled, trembled, and twisted in agony, falling to his knees, only to be jerked back on his feet time and time again . . . bouts of vomiting, tremors, seizures, and fainting fits occurred at varying intervals," until, at the conclusion of the bloody work, he was reduced to "an exhausted, mangled mass of flesh with a craving for water."[36]

Bucklin noted the "series of traumatic injuries" on the back image, extending from the area of the shoulder to the lower portion of the back, the buttocks, and the backs of the calves. Like nearly all Shroud researchers, he concluded that the marks had been made "by some type of object applied as a whip, leaving dumbbell-shaped imprints in the skin, from which blood has issued." The direction of the injuries "is from lateral towards medial" (from the side towards the center of the body), and thus suggests that the whip was applied by someone standing behind the victim.[37]

The Shroud shows the front and back of the man's head, but not the top. It is obvious that the victim was wounded in the head. The hair appears clotted with blood, a feature noted as early as the sixteenth century by the nuns who mended the cloth after the fire. Barbet noted that most of the blood seems to have accumulated at the back of the head. This he found consistent with both crucifixion and with a crowning with thorns, since this area would have touched the beam every time the victim drew back his head during the ordeal, driving the thorns deeper into the scalp and provoking additional bleeding.[38] Several streams of blood make their way down from the top of the forehead towards the eyes. Sebastiano Rodante identified one particular clot on the forehead as arterial blood and a second as blood from the veins.[39] British journalist, Shroud scholar, and art historian Ian Wilson noted eight or more rivulets "each expanding and sometimes dividing along the way," sometimes "interrupted by some obstruction."[40] Barbet noted that the flows of flood on the front of the head were less copious than those on the back, but easier to discern. "There are . . . some coming from the top of the cranium and there is a long trail on each of the thick masses of hair that frame the face. There are four or five which start from the top of the forehead, moving down towards the face." One of them was "so striking and true to life" that the surgeon wrote, "I simply cannot imagine such a one being portrayed by a painter." It begins high up, at the hairline, with one of the apparent thorn-wounds, then "moves down to the medial part of the left superciliary arch, following a meandering course obliquely downwards and outwards. It broadens progressively, just as a flow of blood does on a wounded man when it meets with obstacles."[41]

The bleeding on the head appears to have been caused by many small puncture wounds[42] consistent with a cap of thorns. Cameron observed that "the multiple puncture marks with attendant rivulets of blood over the scalp, extending from the centre of the forehead towards the front round to the level of the ears at the back of head, would suggest a clump of thorny twigs being pressed upon the head."[43] This would be slightly different from the circlet or wreath of thorns usually depicted in sacred art.

Bucklin similarly noted, in the image of the face, "a ring of puncture tracks" involving the scalp. "One of these has the configuration of a number '3.' Blood has issued from these punctures into the hair and onto the skin of the forehead." The image of the back of the victim reveals that the puncture wounds extend around the back of the scalp like a crown. "The direction of the blood flow, both anterior and posterior, is downward."[44]

Baden insisted that "when the scalp bleeds, it doesn't flow in rivulets; the blood mats on the hair."[45] Bucklin responded to this remark by asserting that the Shroud image does in fact show "matting at the back of the head" and insisting, that in his experience, "A sharp pointed instrument would cause a blood flow from the scalp, as it appears on the Shroud."[46]

Zugibe, who saw evidence of a crown or cap of thorns, noted that the scalp is rich in blood vessels and is also supplied by branches of the trigeminal nerve (in the front of the head) and the occipital nerve (in the back). The thorns would have cut into the scalp and blows from the soldiers, as well as simply walking, would surely have irritated these nerves, causing "severe pains resembling a hot poker or electric shock lancinating across the sides of [the victim's] face or deep to his ears." The pain would stop abruptly, but return "with the slightest movement of the jaws or even from a wisp of wind."[47]

Baden alone failed ot see facial wounds. "It's all in the mind of the beholder,"[48] he insisted. Most observers have noted a large swelling below the right eye, a swollen nose, a triangular-shaped mark on the right cheek, and swelling around both eyebrows.[49] Bucklin noted "a distinct abrasion at the tip of the nose" and a "distinctly swollen" right cheek. [50] When the Shroud was taken from its container and examined by scientists in 1978, on the part of the Shroud where the nose is represented, particles of "skin residue" and dust were found, as if the man had injured himself by an unbroken fall on his face.[51] Bucklin also discerned in the midline of the forehead "a square imprint giving the appearance of an object resting on the skin." Although both eyes appear to be closed, "on very close inspection," he wrote, "rounded foreign objects can be noted on the imprint in the area of the right and left eyes."[52] Cameron, who was unable to discern any objects over the eyes, stated that the facial injuries were consistent with the "victim either being struck in the face or falling on the face."[53]

The arms of the victim are bent across the lower abdomen. The fact that they obscure the pelvic area has provoked comment. Some who believe that the Shroud is a medieval forgery point to the prudery of the putative artist as the reason why the intimate parts of the victim are not in evidence. However, the pathologists who have studied the Shroud find nothing unusual. Cameron wrote that the arms would have been forced into that position "in order to break the . . . muscle stiffening of the shoulder-girdle — a not unusual problem when dealing with death from any cause, in order to get the body into a straight position."[54] Archaeologists who excavated a cemetery in Israel which dates to the time of Christ and earlier noted a number of skeletons with the hands crossed over the pelvis, in the same position as the man of the Shroud.[55]

Bucklin wrote, "By examination of the arms, forearms, wrists, and hands, the pathologist notes that the left hand overlies the right wrist. On the left wrist area is a distinct puncture-type injury which has two projecting rivulets [of blood] derived from a central source and separated by about a ten-degree angle." These rivulets extend in a horizontal direction. "The pathologist realizes," Bucklin continues, "that this blood flow could not have happened with the arms in the position as he sees them during his examination, and he must reconstruct the position of the arms in such a way as to place them where they would have to be to account for gravity in the direction of the blood flow." These calculations indicated "that the arms would have to be outstretched upward at about a sixty-five degree angle with the horizontal." He also observed blood flows extending from the wrists towards the elbows on both forearms, and accounted for them "by the position of the arms . . . just determined."[56]

Ian Wilson, who wrote several books and articles about the Shroud, observed that two "separately angled blood flows," one broad and the other long and thin, can be seen on the left wrist, then, after a gap of a few centimeters, he notes that at least six blood rivulets appear to flow into the elbow joint. Although the right wrist is obscured by the left, the presence of similar bloodstains on this arm suggest that they originated in an injury similar to that of the left wrist. "Each rivulet of blood ends with its course pointing in a specific direction, from which it can be calculated that when the majority of the rivulets flowed, [the victim's] arms must have been at an angle of sixty-five degrees from the vertical — i.e. clearly a crucifixion position."[57]

Mark Borkan, a student of mathematics at Duke University in the early 1990s who studied nearly all available literature on the Shroud, observed that the "two divergent blood flows on each of the arms of the man on the Shroud correspond to the two positions a body can assume on the cross: erect, with the weight of the body on the feet, and sagging, with the weight on the wrists."[58] The two primary positions the arms would assume on the cross, he pointed out, were approximately "fifty-five and sixty-five degrees from vertical" and the "jagged flows of the left forearm would result from the constant up-down movement of the crucified individual."[59]

Cameron likewise was convinced that "the track of the blood rivulets from the nail-marks of the wrists indicate fluctuation in the degree of sagging of the body on the cross. . . . This varied from fifty-five to sixty-five degrees approximately."[60]

Zugibe, however, disagreed with Bucklin, Wilson, and others, and argued that divergent blood flows on the arms were not the result of two positions on the cross, but from the position of the corpse after it was removed from the cross, in which the arms were likely "lowered after discharging clots of dried blood, thereby causing an oozing of the fluid of the blood."[61]

Nearly all the forensic experts who have studied the Shroud have agreed with Bucklin that the victim was evidently nailed through the wrists, not in the center of the hands. Pierre Barbet, who experimented extensively with cadavers, found that if a victim were crucified by means of nails driven through the center of the hands, the weight of the body would cause the nails to rip through the flesh so that the arms would tear off the cross.[62] Zugibe was convinced that the nails were driven at the bottom of the palm, at a place called the "thenar eminence," the "bulky prominence" that extends into the hand from the base of the thumb to the wrist.[63] This area is very strong and a nail could be driven there without breaking bones.

One interesting feature of the image is that the thumbs appear to be drawn up under the hands. "As he examines the fingers," Bucklin wrote, "he notes that both the right and left hands have left imprints of only four fingers. The thumbs are not clearly obvious. This flexion of the thumb towards the palm suggested to the pathologist that there had been some injury to the nerves of the hand."[64] Zugibe, while conceding that there was surely damage to the major nerves of the hand, was convinced that the apparently thumblessness of the man of the Shroud was not due to nerve damage, but to "a relatively natural postmortem position." He noted that many of the corpses received at his medical examiner's office were delivered with their wrists tied so that the hands were crossed, and "in every case the thumbs are in a position in front and slightly to the side of the index fingers." Thus, he concluded, "It would be almost impossible to have impressions of the thumbs because the Shroud would not be in contact with them except for a slight segment at the base of the hand."[65] Barbet and Zugibe both identify the median nerve as the nerve damaged by the nail. Barbet, who served as a surgeon on the battlefield during World War I, noted that injury to this nerve produces "one of the worst tortures imaginable,"[66] as "an inexpressible pain," darting "like lightning" through the fingers, surging up the shoulder "like a trail of fire" to "burst" in the unfortunate victim's brain.[67] Zugibe described the pain as "a peculiar burning sensation that is so intense that even gentle contacts like clothing or air draft cause utter torture. . . . The pain would have been unrelenting and brutal. . . . All the known irritating factors were present to aggravate the condition, including movements of air, the direct sun rays, the heat, the pressure of the nail constantly rubbing against the nerve and the movement of the body on the cross."[68] Normally, only surgery to cut the sympathetic nerves can relieve the pain in patients with damage to the median nerve. Before such surgery was available, people with such an injury frequently became addicted to pain-killers or committed suicide.[69]

Another peculiarity of the hands is that the bones are evident, as if in an x-ray. Most scientists have attributed this to an effect called "de-gloving," the result of "an early post-mortem drying effect,"[70] caused by loss of blood in the hands. Cameron attributed this phenomenon either to loss of blood or "post-mortem change."[71] Zugibe, on the other hand, felt that "the apparent lengthening of the fingers" was simply due to the fact that fingers were compressed by the six-inch domed nail that was commonly used in crucifixions.[72] Physicist John P. Jackson offered another theory to account for the skeletal appearance of the hands that we will take up in a later chapter.

The knees of the Shroud victim show cuts and bruises consistent with one or more falls. The right knee seems injured more severely than the left.[73] Barbet noted that the skin seemed to be torn off both knees, especially the right one, where in the region of the knee-cap he observed "a number of excoriations which vary in size and shape, and have jagged edges." Moreover, "a little above and on the outer side" he found two small, round wounds.[74]

On the posterior image are marks which have been identified as injuries caused by carrying a heavy object. Zugibe observed, "Two images, in the region of the right shoulder blade and right back, suggest bruises which some individuals have related to the carrying of the cross."[75] Bucklin noted over the shoulder blade areas on both sides "an abrasion or denuding of the skin surfaces, consistent with a heavy object, like a beam, resting over the shoulder blades and producing a rubbing effect on the skin surfaces."[76] Barbet noted that on the right shoulder, in the outer part of the area below the shoulder blade, there was a broad area where the skin seemed to have been scraped away. These "excoriations" appeared to be "superimposed" on the wounds from the flogging, "which seem to be, as it were, bruised and widened by them." The surgeon wrote, "It would appear that some weighty body, and one with a furrowed surface and which was badly fastened, must have lain on this shoulder and have bruised, reopened, and widened the wounds of the scourging through the [victim's] tunic."[77] Those who believe that the image is that of Jesus assume that this injury was caused by the cross that He was forced to carry to His execution.

The posterior imprint of the body conveys information concerning the condition of the feet. Bucklin noted that "there is a reasonably clear outline of the right foot made by the sole of that foot having been covered with blood and leaving an imprint which reflects the heel as well as the toes. The left foot imprint is less clear and it is also noticeable that the left calf imprint is unclear." This, the pathologist argued, "supports the opinion that the left leg had been rotated and crossed over the right instep in such a way that an incomplete foot print was formed." Bucklin also noted "a definite puncture defect" in the center of the imprint of the right foot. The puncture, he found, was "consistent with an object having penetrated the structures of the feet, and from the position of the feet, the conclusion would be reasonable that the same object penetrated both feet after the left foot had been placed over the right."[78]

Zugibe also observed that the right foot appears more clearly than the left in the image and noted what appeared to be a nail wound in the center of the foot. He felt, however, that the transfixion of both feet by one nail was only one possibility. "The fact that the left foot appears shorter and the right foot slants slightly inward could also suggest that a fold [in the cloth] in a diagonal direction above the heel is possible. The other possibility is that the right foot was nailed flush to the upright and the left foot not completely flush. When cadaveric spasm and subsequent rigor mortis set in, only the right foot may have been flush to the Shroud with the left foot somewhat raised."[79] The nail, Zugibe was convinced, would have wounded the plantar nerves, causing severe pain, like a wound from a red-hot poker. Even a slight movement would cause "incessant, burning cramps," as well as numbness and coldness.[80]

Jackson, noting that the blood trickle seen on the image of the back of the foot matches exactly that corresponding bloodstain on the front image, concluded, "This cannot be coincidence, nor the result of a super-sophisticated artist who anticipated such a detail."[81]

A large, dark splotch on the left side of the front image beside one of the patched places indicates to most trained observers that the man of the Shroud was wounded on the right side of his body, between his fifth and sixth ribs, a few inches below the nipple. Baden saw nothing there but "an area of darkening" and denied that there was evidence of "any discrete injury on the chest."[82] Other pathologists saw this area as clearly indicative of a wound which caused a heavy flow of blood, which is visible on the dorsal image, dripping across the entire small of the back.[83] The dimensions of the wound correspond exactly to the sort of wound caused by the lance that Roman soldiers carried in the first century. Archaeologists have noted that some surviving specimens of the Roman *lancea*, seen in cross section, match perfectly the dimensions of the Shroud wound.[84]

Bucklin, noting the large blood-stain over the right pectoral area, wrote, "Close examination shows a variance in intensity of the stain consistent with the presence of two types of fluid, one comprised of blood, and the other resembling water." He pointed out that there was "distinct evidence of a gravitational effect on this stain, with the blood flowing downward and without spatter or other evidence of projectile activity which would be expected from blood issuing from a functional arterial source." The wound, he observed, "has all the characteristics of a postmortem type of flow of blood from a body cavity or from an organ such as the heart." At the "upper plane of the wound," he indicated, was an egg-shaped "skin defect . . . characteristic of a penetrating track produced by a sharp puncturing instrument."[85] Bucklin went on to say that the image of the pectoral area "suggests to the forensic pathologist that the puncturing instrument released a watery type fluid from the body cavities as well as blood from the heart area. One potential consideration would be that there was fluid in the chest cavity which was released by the penetrating instrument and this was followed by blood issuing from an area as the result of the heart being perforated."[86]

Zugibe essentially described the wound as between the fifth and sixth ribs, with the right side of the wound about six inches from the center of the chest and the left lower side of the wound positioned about two-and-a-quarter inches from the breastbone. The large smudge of blood below the wound indicated to him that "shortly after the spear thrust, blood ran down the side of the chest, drying and clotting. Then, when [the body] was removed from the cross and placed on the Shroud, some of the liquid blood oozed out of the large wound to the back, causing the horizontal streams."[87] Barbet concluded that the position of the wound suggests that the lance penetrated the right auricle of the heart and the pericardial sac that surrounds it.[88]

Cameron was also convinced that the lance entered the chest cavity "in an upward, inward direction," and penetrated the right lung, causing it to collapse and provoking a hemorrhage into the chest cavity. Such a wound, he said, "could well" penetrate the right side of the heart and, in a living person, cause "almost immediate death."[89]

When tests were performed on the Shroud, traces of serous fluid were detected along with the blood. Some medical experts believed that the fluid came from the pericardial sac; others thought it came from the pleural sac; all agreed that the clear fluid "was a part of the postmortem issue of blood and clear fluid resulting from a puncture wound that reached the heart."[90]

What was the exact cause of death? Many assume that victims of crucifixion died from loss of blood, but this was seldom the case. The Roman soldiers who routinely carried out the procedure made sure that no major arteries were severed. Hermann Moedder, an Austrian radiologist working in Cologne, Germany, attributed death to "orthostatic collapse." In other words, the position of the victim on the cross caused his blood to pool in the lower parts of the body, starving the heart and brain.[91]

Orazio Petrosillo, an Italian journalist, and Emanuela Marinelli, the founder of a Shroud research group in Rome, in their 1990 book *La Sindone* expressed their belief that the man of the Shroud died of a phenomenon known as "haemopericardium," or blood in the area around the heart. Severe stress, they argue, can put such a strain on the heart muscle (even in a young, healthy subject) that the pericardium is flooded with blood. "The violent dilatation of the membranes causes the patient to emit a loud cry [as is recorded of Jesus], due to a lacerating pain behind the sternum, and to die almost immediately afterwards. The rapid death, which occurs when the individual is completely lucid, during a violent physical effort and in a state of great tiredness, normally causes that immediate cadaveric rigidity which anatomopathologists call 'statuary rigidity' and which easily explains the position of the body as it is observed on the Shroud."[92]

Robert Bucklin wrote, "A detailed study of the Shroud imprint and the blood stains, coupled with a basic understanding of the physical and physiological changes in the body that take place during crucifixion, suggests strongly that the decedent [dead man] had undergone postural asphyxia as a result of his position during the crucifixion episode." In other words, he suffocated. The pathologist also noted evidence of "severe blood loss from the skin wounds as well as fluid accumulation in the chest cavities [because of diminished respiratory capacity] related to terminal cardio-respiratory failure."[93]

Bucklin was in essential agreement with Barbet, who noted that there is often a *hydropericardium*, or a copious accumulation of fluid in the area around the heart in a person who has suffered a painful, traumatic death.[94] Bucklin also agreed with the French surgeon in his belief that the victim died of asphyxiation. Barbet pointed out that crucifixion caused cramps and contractions known as "tetany," which eventually spread to the chest muscles and prevented the victim from emptying his lungs.[95] Completely convinced that the man depicted on the Shroud was Jesus, in a meditation called "The Corporeal Passion of Jesus Christ," Barbet described this phenomenon in poignant detail: "The muscles of His arms stiffen of themselves, in a contraction which becomes more and more accentuated; His deltoid muscles and His biceps become strained and stand out, His fingers are drawn sharply inwards . . . on His thighs and on His legs there are monstrous rigid bulges, and His toes are bent. It is like a wounded man suffering from tetanus, a prey to those horrible spasms, which once seen can never be forgotten. It is what we describe as *tetanisation*, when the cramps become generalised. . . . The stomach muscles become tightened in set undulations, then [the muscles around the ribs], then the muscles of the neck, then the respiratory. His breathing has gradually become shorter and lighter. His sides, which have already been drawn upwards by the traction of the arms, are now exaggeratedly so; the solar plexus sinks inwards, and so do the hollows under the collar-bone. The air enters with a whistling sound, but scarcely comes out any longer. He is breathing in the upper regions only. He breathes in a little, but cannot breathe out. He thirsts for air . . . like someone in the throes of asthma. . . . A flush has gradually spread over His pale face; it has turned a violet purple and then blue. He is *asphyxiating*."[96]

Hermann Moedder, the radiologist from Cologne, experimented with medical students who volunteered to be suspended by the wrists. He found that the capacity of the lungs decreased from 5.2 to 1.5 liters, the breathing became more shallow and rapid, the chest circumference remained fixed. The volunteers would have suffocated had they not been allowed to stand three minutes in alternation with three minutes of hanging. He theorized that a victim of crucifixion would have to raise himself periodically on his pierced feet to keep from asphyxiating and that eventually, overcome by exhaustion and unable to pull himself up anymore, he would succumb to "orthostatic collapse," when the blood pooled in the lower parts of his body and starved his heart.[97] Frederick Zugibe disagreed, suggesting that the victim's arms were extended to the sides rather than fixed above the head, and he conducted his own experiments, attaching volunteers to a cross with the arms outstretched, a fashion consistent with his studies of the man of the Shroud. The volunteers showed no signs of suffocation. Neither Moedder nor Zugibe, of course, *nailed* their volunteers, and conducted their experiments under conditions which would not cause injury. While conceding several possible causes of death, Zugibe wrote that the most likely cause was "shock" — in which the body is deprived of oxygen because of a sharp decrease in the flow of the blood to the tissues. The man of the Shroud, he said, suffered first of all from *traumatic shock* — the result of physical injury and pain. Secondly, he also suffered from what is known as *hypvolemic shock*. This would have resulted when bleeding and perspiration lowered the volume of the victim's blood and caused his blood pressure to plummet. Moreover, the victim also suffered *cardiogenic shock*. This would have ensued when the blood of the victim, immobile on the cross, began to pool in the legs, as the blood pressure dropped to the point that the heart failed to pump properly and caused fluid to accumulate in the lungs and the spaces around them. If Zugibe were to fill out a death certificate for the man on the Shroud, he would list the cause of death as "cardiac and respiratory arrest due to severe pulmonary edema due to cardiogenic, traumatic, and hypovolemic shock due to crucifixion."[98]

The image on the Shroud is of a fairly young man (the age is estimated at between thirty and forty-five) of Middle Eastern appearance who has been scourged, crowned with thorns, crucified, and killed. The surgeons and pathologists who have studied the image have found the wounds completely realistic. Does this mean that this is necessarily the image of Jesus Christ? Crucifixion was, as we have seen, a very common means of executing criminals during the first centuries of the Christian era. There were thousands — perhaps even millions — of crucifixion victims during the six-hundred-year period in which this form of torture was practiced. Many victims of crucifixion were scourged before they were nailed through the hands and feet. Many, like the man of the Shroud, were forced to carry part of their cross.

There are, however, some features of the image on the Shroud that are specifically in common with the crucifixion of Jesus, as it is described in the Gospels. First, there is the severity of the scourging. As we have seen, prisoners condemned to die were normally not beaten so badly as the man of the Shroud. The Gospels report that Pilate evidently caused Jesus to be flogged into a pitiable condition in an effort to quiet calls for His execution. In fact, a physician who wrote about the death of Jesus in the *Journal of the American Medical Association* believed that Jesus was possibly in what would now be termed "critical' condition after the scourging.[99]

A second feature the man on the Shroud has specifically in common with Jesus is that he has worn a crown of thorns. This was not a usual means of torture. The Roman soldiers tortured Him in this way because He was accused of trying to make Himself king of the Jews. Even so, this does not preclude the possibility that, among the myriads of nameless wretches who, throughout the ages, underwent crucifixion, *no one* else was tortured with a crown of thorns.

Third, there is evidence of a flow of clear fluid from the area around the heart in connection to a lance wound through the heart after death. As we have seen, William Meacham, the archaeologist, believed that this was not a normal way to dispatch a prisoner, but his comments are in the way of speculation, based on the comments of an ancient theological writer who may or may not have been familiar with the actual process of crucifixion. Sufficient historical documentation does not exist to assert the claim with any firmness. Therefore, before we can further consider an identification of the Shroud victim with Jesus, we must first see what the Scriptures relate about His death and burial.

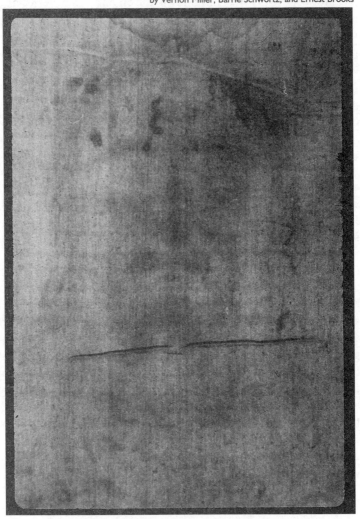

A close-up photo of the face on the shroud.

Chapter III

The Bible and the Shroud

We shall now see what the Bible has to say about the death and burial of Jesus with reference to the features on the Shroud. The details of the Passion of Jesus are recorded in the Gospels of Matthew, Mark, Luke, and John, and tend to be accepted even by liberals who reject much of the other things that are recounted about Jesus. To what extent do the accounts of the evangelists corroborate or contradict the record of the suffering of the man on the Shroud?

St. Matthew tells us that Pontius Pilate, the Roman governor of Judaea, aware that "it was out of envy" that the "chief priests and elders" of Jerusalem were trying to secure the condemnation of Jesus, called to their attention the custom by which, on the Feast of Passover, the Roman authorities would release any one prisoner whose freedom was requested by the people of the city. He then suggested that they request the liberation of the Nazarene. When instead they insisted on the release of Barabbas — described by Mark and Luke as a terrorist — Pilate, fearing a riot, washed his hands to protest his innocence of responsibility for the death of a guiltless man. Then, after having Him scourged, he handed Him over to his soldiers for death by crucifixion (see Mt 27:24-26).

St. Mark, in a much shorter account, says the same thing as St. Matthew (see Mk 15:6-15). St. Luke recounts that Pilate, whose jurisdiction was the area around Jerusalem, when he learned that Jesus was a resident of the district to the north, sent the prisoner to Herod, tetrarch of Galilee, in an attempt to "pass the buck," only to have the tetrarch send Him back to Jerusalem again. Like Matthew and Mark, Luke tells us that Pilate did not want to condemn Jesus. Twice the governor tried to bargain with the angry mob, declaring that he would "punish" Jesus and then release Him, but when the crowd insisted on crucifixion, he gave in (see Lk 23:1-25).

St. John corroborates the accounts of the other evangelists, describing Pilate's attempts to free Jesus and his fear of the Jewish leaders. Whereas we learn from Luke that Pilate told Jesus' enemies that he would "punish" him and then release him, St. John tells us that Pilate did in fact have Jesus flogged (see Jn 19:1). When Pilate presented his bleeding and mangled victim to the bloodthirsty crowd, insisting that he had found no basis for a charge against Him (see Jn 19:4), the mob continued to clamor for crucifixion, and after additional frantic persuasion failed, the governor, with the backbone of a chocolate eclair, ordered the crucifixion of Jesus (see Jn 19:2-16).

Thus the Scriptures indicate that Pilate, who knew that Jesus was innocent of the charges of sedition brought against Him, ordered an unusually severe beating. This is consistent with the evidence of more than one hundred lashes on the body of the man whose image appears on the Shroud. That number of stripes was far in excess of the usual practice, and many are convinced that Pilate ordered an unusually brutal flogging in hopes that, seeing Jesus whipped to a bloody pulp, His enemies would cease to insist upon His death.

The Shroud victim was forced to wear a cap of thorns. In Matthew we are told that the soldiers platted a crown of thorns (see

Mt 27:29). John likewise tells us, "And the soldiers plaited a crown of thorns, and put it on his head. . ." (Jn 19:2). Scripture does not tell us how the crown was shaped. The crowns worn by some kings and princes were wreath-like circlets, while others were like caps or turbans — the shape of the gruesome headgear inflicted on the man of the Shroud."

Jesus, in traditional art, is shown carrying His entire cross. Tradition also holds that He fell several times while being taken to His place of execution. The man on the Shroud evidently carried a heavy beam across his shoulders and his knees bear evidence of at least one fall. St. John states that "Jesus . . . went out, bearing his own cross" (Jn 19:17). Matthew, Mark, and Luke do not state specifically that Jesus was made to carry His cross, but all record that the Roman soldiers grabbed a man from the crowd — Simon from Cyrene (in North Africa) — and made him carry the cross, clearly implying that, up until that moment, Jesus had been bearing it. We are not told anything about the physical form or shape of the cross — whether He carried part of it or the whole thing — nor are we told that Jesus fell at any time. The fact, however, that Jesus *went out* carrying His cross and that at some point His executioners forced someone else to carry it for Him would indicate that something had happened to convince them that Jesus was physically incapable of carrying it any longer.

The man of the Shroud was nailed through the wrist area and through the feet. All four Gospels simply state that Jesus was "crucified." After the Resurrection the apostle Thomas, informed that in his absence Jesus had appeared to other disciples, insisted, "Unless I see in his hands the print of the nails, and place my finger in the mark of the nails . . . I will not believe" (Jn 20:25). The comment sheds no light as to specifically where on the hand Jesus was nailed. The part of the wrist where the man of the Shroud was nailed could easily be described as a part of the hand. Thomas does not mention wounds in the feet, but his omission does not mean that Jesus was nailed through the hands only. St. John, equating Jesus with the passover lamb, of which no bones were to be broken, recounts that his Master suffered no broken bones (see Jn 19:36; Ex12:46; Nm 9:12). There is no evidence from the

Shroud that the man whose image appears there, despite massive injury, suffered any broken bones.

John records that when Jesus' executioners decided not to break His legs, to make absolutely sure that He was dead, they pierced His side with a spear, causing a flow of blood and water (see Jn 19:34). The man on the Shroud was indeed stabbed through the side, and, as we have seen, there is evidence not only of a flow of blood but of clear fluid as well.

The Gospels do not provide any detail about the symptoms of Jesus' death agony, except that He said that He was thirsty (see Jn 19:28) — which would have been the normal consequence of the sweating and blood loss associated with His ordeal. If, in fact, He eventually suffocated, during His three-hour ordeal He was able to speak, briefly, at least seven times.

After Jesus' death was confirmed, St. Matthew tells us that a rich disciple named Joseph of Arimathea made a successful request of Pontius Pilate for the body, which he then wrapped in a clean linen cloth and placed in his own tomb, which had been cut out of rock (see Mt 27:57-60). St. Mark and St. Luke record the same events. St. John provides the added detail that another disciple, Nicodemus, brought a mixture of myrrh and aloes weighing about seventy-five pounds, and along with Joseph wrapped the body with the spices in the burial clothing, in accordance with Jewish burial customs (see Jn 19:39-40). Students of the Shroud have debated as to whether the body was washed. Most have assumed that it was not, because of the presence of bloodstains. Scripture does not say that the body of Jesus was washed, but Jewish custom stipulated that prior to burial corpses were to be washed seven times. Some have argued that Jesus' followers did not have time to perform this ritual, since it was probably close to sundown by the time that the body was recovered and this marked the beginning of the Sabbath, when no labor could be performed. Josh McDowell, the author of several books explaining the Christian faith, disagreed and wrote, "The idea of there not being time to wash the body clean with water because of the approaching Sabbath is . . . weak because the Scripture says they still had time to anoint the body with over a hundred pounds of spices." Moreover, he pointed out, the Mishnah permitted the washing and anointing of a corpse on the Sabbath, so long as the limbs were not "strained out of joint."[100]

However, the *Code of Jewish Law,* which was written down in the sixteenth century but which records practices which date, according to some Jewish scholars, to the first century and earlier, a different procedure was used for victims of violent, bloody death. First of all, they were not to be washed, because of the belief that the entire body, including spilled blood, should be kept together to ensure resurrection.[101] Furthermore, in such cases, a one-piece shroud was commonly used, rather than linen strips, which might permit the escape of trickles of life-blood.[102]

Zugibe, on the other hand, was convinced that the body imaged on the Shroud had to have been washed, otherwise the cloth would have been saturated with gore and "would bear large, indistinct masses of blood over the face, hand, arm, feet, and trunk." Saturation of the cloth with blood would have interfered with the formation of the face and body images in the affected areas of the cloth. Zugibe believed that if the body had been washed briefly prior to placement in the Shroud, the blood would have oozed slightly out of the wounds, as he observed routinely in cases of violent death, and caused imprints consistent with those of the Shroud."[103]

According to the Mishnah, a body had to be washed seven times and the hair and beard completely shaven at burial.[104] Obviously this was not the case with the man whose image appears on the Shroud. Since the Sabbath occurred at sundown — approximately three hours after Jesus' death — it has been argued by some that by the time Jesus' family and friends had secured the body there was no time for the customary preparations, except for a hasty anointing with spices and perhaps, as Zugibe believed, a single hurried washing.

Optical crystallographer Joseph Kohlbeck presented evidence in 1986 that the man of the Shroud had been placed in a rock-hewn tomb. Obtaining samples of limestone from ancient tombs in and around Jerusalem, he subjected them to microscopic analysis and found "travertine aragonite deposited from springs, as well as small quantities of iron and strontium." Then he examined a particle taken from the Shroud in the area of the foot. Here he found aragonite as well as strontium and iron, which proved to be "an unusually close match" to the samples from the Jerusalem cave tombs.[105]

At question is the exact meaning of the Greek word used for the linen in which Jesus' body was enfolded. Matthew tells us that Joseph of Arimathea took Jesus' body and wrapped it in a linen Shroud (see Mt 27:59-60). The Greek word usually translated as shroud is *sindon*. In the literature of the time, it usually refers to the type of winding sheet of which the Shroud of Turin is representative. The author of the first Gospel makes no mention as to what became of this cloth after the Resurrection. Mark, likewise, tells us that the body of Jesus was wrapped in a linen shroud, and again, the Greek word is *sindon*. Like Matthew, Mark does not mention the *sindon* after the Resurrection. Luke also records that Jesus' corpse was wrapped in a *sindon*. However, when Peter is described as finding the linen lying by itself after the Resurrection (see Lk 24:12), the word used is *othonia*, which is plural, and has occasioned nearly all translators to render it as "linen cloths" or "linen wraps." John speaks of the body being wrapped also in *othonia* (see Jn 19:40). Then, when he recounts his arrival (or that of "the disciple whom Jesus loved") with Peter at the empty tomb, he says, "Then Simon Peter came, following [John], and went into the tomb; he saw the linen cloths lying, and the napkin, which had been on his head, not lying with the linen cloths but rolled up in a place by itself" (Jn 20:6-7). The Greek word usually translated as "napkin" is *sudarion.*

We have two problems. According to John, the grave clothing of Jesus is described in plural. John also specifies that the body of his Lord was wrapped in two types of graveclothes: the *othonia* (linen cloths) and the *sudarion* (napkin).

Some have said that *othonia* refers to strips like those in which the Egyptians wrapped their mummies. Many artists throughout the years have pictured Jesus as being buried this way. Others have said that *othonia* is to be understood as a "collective singular," just like the English word "clothes" could refer to one article of clothing, or two or three or four. Certainly Luke uses both the singular *sindon* and the plural *othonia* to refer, evidently, to the same thing. Victor Tunkel of the University of London described in a lecture in 1983 how Jewish victims of violent death were usually buried in one-piece shrouds. Petrosillo and Marinelli cite the instance of a skeleton of an individual buried in such a way which was found in 1951 in Israel, at Khirbet Qumrum. They do not identify the century of the burial, however, or cite their source for this information.[106]

However, what is to be made of St. John's assertion that Jesus' burial clothing was in two parts? Most scholars think that *othonia* refers to what we now know as the Shroud, or something similar. The *sudarion* was most likely a smaller cloth put over the face or tied around it to keep the mouth from falling open.

Some have seen indications on the Shroud that the man's head was bound with a jaw-band.[107] One such person was English bishop and Biblical scholar John A.T. Robinson, famous for his book *Honest to God*, who pointed out what appeared to him to be a dark band under the chin of the man on the Shroud. This feature looked "as if it is where the jaw-band has retracted a portion of the beard which would otherwise show up." Moreover, he claimed that "the vertical strips on each side of the face between the cheeks and the [hair], otherwise solid, could similarly be caused by the band holding back the intervening hair. The band would then continue up in front of the ears and under the hair which grows from the front part of the beard, thus forcing it into prominence. It would then join over the crown of the head at the back, causing the 'pinched' effect by which the head narrows to a point at the top."[108] Other observers, however, have concluded that the dark band that Robinson observed was simply a feature of the cloth and not the image.

In the cathedral of Oviedo in Spain there is preserved a piece of cloth, two feet nine inches by one foot nine inches, called *El Sudario*, which is supposed to be the cloth which covered the face of the dead Christ.[109] Vatican archivist Giulio Ricci studied it in 1955 and noticed similarities between its bloodstains and the stains around the head of the man of the Shroud.[110] In the 1980s it was studied by Dr. Alan Whanger, professor of psychiatry at Duke University, who along with his wife Mary developed the technique of the "polarized image." This technique, originally used to compare works of art, involves the use of polarized filters to separate ordinary light into light waves in which the axes are aligned along a single plane, allowing for detailed comparisons of two images. Using this technique, the Whangers compared *El Sudario* with the Shroud and found "a remarkable correspondence" between the bloodstains on the two cloths.[111] The dorsal head wounds on the two cloths were compared, and the similarity of the two complex patterns was clear enough to suggest that the two cloths were in contact with the same body, presumably within a short time period.[112]

According to a history of *El Sudario* written in the 1100s, this cloth was kept in Jerusalem until shortly before the city was conquered by the Persians in the seventh century, when it was taken first to Alexandria and then to Spain, where it was kept in several locations before finding a home in the cathedral of Oviedo. It was mentioned in an eleventh-century list of relics kept there.[113] Max Frei, a Swiss criminologist who, as we shall see in a later chapter, studied samples of pollen on the Shroud, found on *El Sudario* pollen from all the areas mentioned in the twelfth-century chronicle, and no place else.[114] Max Guscin, of the British Society for the Turin Shroud, contended that the stains on *El Sudario* coincided exactly with the shape and form of the face of the man of the Shroud, and that the length of the nose is precisely eight centimeters on both cloths.[115]

Some have questioned why, if the image of Jesus was actually imprinted on His burial clothes, this fact is not mentioned in the New Testament. It seems clear, however, that the apostles who authored the Gospels and epistles were interested, above all, in spreading the message of salvation through Jesus Christ. They were not interested in providing any facts about His life that were not related to the essence of His teaching. To call attention to a piece of cloth that preserved His physical appearance might have been a distraction.

There are two specific reasons why the apostles may have been extremely reluctant to display the linen. First, Jews were forbidden (see Ex 20:4-6) to make likenesses of any living being. An image of Jesus on a burial cloth, even if of supernatural origin, besides being "unclean" because of contact with the dead, would surely be denounced as an idol and its display would injure the credibility of the apostles in their attempt to draw the devout Jewish countrymen to the faith.

Second, even apart from the image, the apostles may have found veneration of the Shroud spiritually dangerous. For example, Hezekiah, one of the godly kings of ancient Israel, upon his accession "broke in pieces the bronze serpent that Moses had made, for until those days the people of Israel had burned incense to it" (2 Kings 18:4). During their wanderings in the wilderness, the people of Israel, because of their unbelief and rebellion against God, were bitten by poisonous snakes. Moses was directed by God to make a statue of a snake and put it on a pole, "and if a serpent bit any man, he would look at the bronze serpent and live" (Nm 21:8). The bronze serpent, then, was an important relic, that over the years was misused. When King Hezekiah saw that people were worshiping the brazen serpent, he caused it to be destroyed. It is quite possible that the apostles did not want to have to destroy the Shroud under such circumstances, which could very easily have developed.

The fact is, if one studies the image on the Shroud in light of the New Testament record, it is difficult to find evidence of any injury sustained by the man depicted on the celebrated cloth that fails to correspond to the injuries to Christ described or implied by the evangelists. Likewise there is no detail in the New Testament account of the death and burial of Jesus that clearly contradicts the witness of the Shroud of Turin.

The Della Rovere painting of the shroud.

Chapter IV

The Image Not Made with Hands

Although the Bible does not record the preservation of the Shroud, there are several writings from the early centuries of the Christian era that *seem* to do so. These references are among writings called the *Apocrypha*. The word *apocrypha* comes from Greek words meaning "hidden." The writings are "hidden" because they are not part of the official canon of the Bible. Actually, when we speak of the Apocrypha, we refer to two sets of writing. First, there are fourteen books of the Old Testament which were originally written in Greek, rather than Hebrew, most of them not long before the time of Christ in what scholars call the "intertestamentary period." These books are part of the Bible used by all Roman Catholics and some of the more traditional Protestants. During the Reformation, however, some leaders of the newly formed denominations discarded them as works of dubious authenticity, and thus they do not appear in the Bibles used by many (if not most) Protestants. Nor do these Greek works appear in the Hebrew Bible used by Jews. These Jewish apocryphal writings have no bearing on the Shroud.

There is, however, a second group of books known as Apocrypha which were *never* a part of the biblical canon. Some of them, such as *The Gospel According to Thomas* and *The Gospel According to Peter*, are attributed to apostles, but they never became part of the official text of the New Testament because church officials, at the time when sufficient documentation was in existence to permit such a decision, determined either that they were not written by the people to whom they are attributed (and were therefore forgeries), were composed after the period when the first generation of Christians was active, contained material better expressed in the works that became part of the canon, conveyed incorrect theological positions, or were obviously fictional. It is this second body of works known as Apocrypha that contains a *few* references to the Shroud, or something similar. We can cite them because at this point we are not specifically concerned so much with the accuracy of the facts they convey as in what they call tell us what was commonly believed at the time.

An important reference to the possible existence of the Shroud within a few centuries of the lifetime of Jesus comes from the famous theologian and Church Father St. Jerome, from a work written in Bethlehem in A.D. 392 called *Lives of Illustrious Men*. This is a series of very brief biographical sketches of the various early leaders of the Christian Church. One of the most important leaders was St. James, the Lord's "brother." (Jerome, elsewhere, because of his belief in the perpetual virginity of Mary, makes it clear that James was either the child of an earlier marriage of Joseph or a cousin, but certainly not the biological son of Mary.) A devout and pious man all his life, James, who was a priest at the Temple and scrupulously lived by the Law of Moses until the day of his death, [116] led the Church in Jerusalem until his martyrdom at the hands of hostile Jews in A.D. 62. Jerome, in his *Lives*, cited the apocryphal *Gospel According to the Hebrews* (of which no copies have survived), in which it was stated that Jesus, after His Resurrection but before He appeared to James (Paul, in 1 Corinthians 15, tells us that the Lord did in fact appear to James), gave His graveclothes "to the servant of the priest."[117] In other words, Jesus gave His Shroud to James' servant. No mention, however, is made of an image on the graveclothes.

St. Nino (sometimes called St. Nina) was a Greek Christian girl, born in Cappadocia (in what is now Turkey) around A.D. 296. Her parents moved to Jerusalem when she was twelve. Later, as a captive, she was taken to what is now Georgia (in southeastern Europe), where she introduced the Christian faith. Shortly before she died in A.D. 338, she dictated her life story to her friend Salome of Ujarma. In the earliest version preserved, which dates to the fifth century, Nino mentions the Shroud. Reminiscing about her early life in Jerusalem, Nino recounted, "And they taught me that the things written by the prophet were fulfilled in the Lord, and that he was crucified and went up into heaven and is to come again. And the [grave] clothes the wife of Pilate asked for . . . and believed in Christ, and deported to Pontus [in what is now Turkey] to her home. And after a time it fell to Luke the Evangelist, and he knows what he did with them. As to the napkin, Peter, they say, took it with him"[118] It is significant that Nino distinguished between the graveclothes and the napkin, or cloth, that covered or went around Jesus' head. It is also noteworthy that she was ignorant of their location at the time she dictated her memoirs.

St. Braulio, bishop of Saragossa, Spain, from 631 until his death twenty years later, mentioned in a letter that the physical "relics" of Jesus were still to be seen in Jerusalem, and were "left to us as a testimony of His passion." Among these was the column to which Jesus was tied while he was being scourged. Braulio went on to state that "the linens and Shroud, in which Our Lord was wrapped, may well have been saved by the Apostles as relics. The fame of such relics alone would assure a good Christian that they were preserved carefully, though dispersed throughout the world."[119] It is evident that Braulio had neither actually seen the Shroud nor was absolutely certain of its survival. They were *not* in Jerusalem in the 600s. Braulio simply stated that the burial clothes *might* have been saved.

There are other references to the preservation of Jesus'

graveclothes. Around 570, a pilgrim to the Holy Land named Antonius of Placentia wrote of seeing a cave on the banks of the Jordan River, where he was told that the Shroud was preserved.[120] He evidently did not see the cloth, and it is not clear whether he believed it was housed there at the time. However, when Arculf, a French bishop who was a contemporary of Braulio of Saragossa, visited Jerusalem around the year 640, he reported seeing relics such as the column to which Jesus had been bound during the scourging (also reported by Braulio), as well as the cup from which Jesus drank (later called "The Holy Grail") and the lance which pierced Jesus' side. He made no mention, however, of anything fitting the description of the Shroud.[121]

One of the first jurisdictions in the world to embrace Christianity was the city-state of Edessa, which is now Urfa in the nation of Turkey. The teachings of Jesus were introduced there in the third or fourth decade of the first century, under King Abgar V, who died in A.D. 50. The fourth-century historian Eusebius, who had access to the archives of Edessa, found documentation of a correspondence between Abgar and Jesus. Abgar at the time was seriously ill and wrote the Nazarene, asking Him to come there to heal him. Jesus sent word that He was unable to come, but promised, "When I have been taken up I will send you one of my disciples to cure your disorder and bring life to you and those with you."[122] Shortly after the resurrection the apostle Thaddeus went to Edessa and cured Abgar. Eusebius does not mention Thaddeus taking the Shroud with him.

Nevertheless, there was a very strong tradition that Thaddeus brought with him a cloth that, in most ways, fits the description of the Holy Shroud. According to *The Doctrine of Addai* (Thaddeus), written around the fourth century (about the same time Eusebius was writing), when Jesus declined to go physically to Abgar, He sent the Edessan ruler a portrait of Himself, painted from life, which the sick king touched, and was healed.[123] The earliest version of *The Acts of Thaddeus* dates from the sixth or seventh century, but many scholars believe that it is based on a text that dates from the third century. It tells a similar story. King Abgar sends a messenger named Ananias to Jesus, charging him "to take accurate account of Christ, of what appearance He was, and His stature, and His hair." When he delivered the letter Ananias stared intently at Jesus, trying to fix in his mind His physical features. Christ, who knew what the messenger was thinking about, announced that He was going to wash Himself. When He did so he handed Ananias the towel with which He had wiped His face — now imprinted with His image — and told him that He was going to send His disciple Thaddeus to enlighten the king and his subjects. It is significant that the towel was, in this narrative, called the "*Tetradiplon*," or "the doubled in four."[124]

A writer named Evagrius Scholasticus, writing shortly after the event, described an attempt by the Persians (who were Zoroastrians) to conquer the Christian city of Edessa by laying siege to it in A.D. 540. Under their leader Chosroes, the Persians constructed a huge mound of earth and timber from which they intended to hurl deadly projectiles onto the defenders of Edessa. The Edessans then tunneled under the mound and crammed the tunnel with wood, which they tried to set on fire to cause the mound to collapse. When, because of insufficient oxygen, the defenders were unable to keep the fire going, Evagrius related, "In this state of utter perplexity, they bring the divinely wrought image, which the hands of men did not form, but Christ our God sent to Abgarus on his desiring to see Him." They took the image into the tunnel, washed the image with water, then sprinkled some water on the timber. When the wood kindled immediately and eventually brought about the desired collapse of the mound, thus frustrating the efforts of Chosroes to take the city, the people of Edessa attributed their deliverance from the Persians to the miraculous image.[125]

This miraculous image was called different things. We have seen that it was sometimes referred to as the "Cloth Folded in Four," or the Tetradiplon. It was often called the "Sacred Mandylion" (*mandylion* is Greek for handkerchief or towel) or the "*Acheiropoietos*," which means "not made with hands." Sometimes it was simply called "The Holy Face" or "The Holy Face of Edessa."

In the sixth century there was a liturgy — or order of service

— in use in Spain, known as the Mozarabic Rite. The *preface* — the words the priest says or sings before consecrating the elements — for Tuesday in Holy Week contains the words: "Peter went with John to the tomb and saw the recent imprints of the dead and risen man on the linens."[126]

The Mandylion was known in Rome in A.D. 769, for in that year Pope Stephen III preached a sermon (of which a twelfth-century copy exists) in which he recounted that Jesus sent word to Abgar, "If you wish to see my human face, here is a linen on which you can see not only the features of my face, but the stature of my whole body divinely formed." Thereupon Jesus lay full length on a snow-white linen cloth "and, wonderful to behold, by an act of God, the glorious features of the Lord and the noble stature of His body were imprinted on it."[127]

So far, we have seen that, according to certain writers from the late Roman/early medieval period, there was an old tradition that the graveclothes that had briefly enshrouded Jesus had somehow been preserved. It seems clear that they were never displayed in Jerusalem along with certain other relics and mementoes of Jesus' earthly life. There was, however, a very strong tradition that a miraculous image of Christ had been taken to Edessa. There was no agreement as to the way in which it was formed, but it was believed to have had a direct connection with Jesus and to bear His true image.

Few would dispute that there was a indeed a cloth kept in the early Middle Ages in Edessa, which was said to bear an authentic portrait of Jesus. Copies of the Mandylion exist, and they all bear an uncanny resemblance to the face on the Shroud. It became the practice of Christians in the Middle East and Eastern Europe to fashion stylized holy pictures, known as icons, and many early examples were supposed to have been copied from the Mandylion. As we shall see in a later chapter, art experts have found many of the features of the Shroud — even some that are merely flaws on the fabric — on icons from the early Middle Ages that are based on the Mandylion. This has led students of the Shroud to conclude that the Mandylion of Edessa was probably one and the same as the Shroud of Turin.[128] But can one know this for sure?

The biggest problem in identifying the Mandylion with the Shroud of Turin is that the Mandylion displayed only the face, not the body. However, as we have seen, another name for the Mandylion was the Tetradiplon, or "the [cloth] folded in four." Ian Wilson took a life-sized copy of the Shroud and folded it in half lengthwise, then in half twice again, and found that on the segment where the head appears that the face appears disembodied (because the neck area on the Shroud is indistinct), just as in the copies of the Mandylion.[129] Wilson also noted that whereas most portraits are tall and narrow, the copies of the Mandylion of Edesssa are all short and wide. There is physical evidence on the Shroud that a side strip was at one time sewn onto one edge, and Wilson speculated that this might have been done so that the image would appear in the center of the frame, rather than to one side.[130] Moreover, physicist John P. Jackson, in his paper "Foldmarks as a Historical Record of the Turin Shroud," based on his own hands-on studies of the Shroud in 1978 and the photographs made at the time, claimed that he found evidence that the Shroud had indeed at one time been folded in eight parts. He said he could pinpoint four old folds with another two "reasonably certain" and "the remainder there by implication." [131]

Why would the Edessans have folded the Shroud so that only the face was evident? Perhaps it was easier to display in that fashion. Some have *speculated* that the first-century Christians felt that the pagans of the time, who could not understand the concept of God (or a god) suffering, on seeing the wounded body of the man they called Lord would only mock the image of a Savior who could not save Himself from suffering and death.[132]

The Roman Empire in Western Europe had long since crumbled into numerous independent and warring states, but for many centuries the Eastern Roman Empire, or the Byzantine Empire, flourished, with its capital at Constantinople (now Istanbul, Turkey). The city-state of Edessa was absorbed into the Empire in the tenth century and forced to surrender its treasured Mandylion. Huge crowds turned out in Constantinople on August 8, 944, to welcome it. The co-emperors Constantine VII Porphyrogenitus and Romanus Lecapenus went to the Golden Gate in the southwest corner of the city, along with the Patriarch and members of the Senate, to escort it to the palace in a triumphal march that proceeded through the length of the city.[133] When the co-emperors viewed the cloth privately, Constantine said he was able to make out the face of a man within the faint stains.[134]

Soon after that, however, the Mandylion must have been taken out of its original frame, because later some witnesses recount that the image included a body as well as a face. Dr. Gino Zaninotto, an Italian historian and archaeologist, found in the Vatican archives the manuscript of a sermon given in the Hagia Sophia (the biggest and most important church in Constantinople) by Gregorius, the Referendary of the Great Church. The sermon was delivered on the evening of August 16, 944, during the ceremony for the enthronement of the image, which had just arrived from Edessa. Gregorius stated, "These are truly things of beauty; they contain the color of the imprint of Christ, which has been further embellished by the drops of blood that gushed from his side."[135] It is clear from this reference that more than the face was then evident. English monk Ordericus Vitalis, in his *Church History* (written around 1141) said that the Mandylion "displayed to those who gazed on it the likeness and proportions of the Lord."[136]

There are several references to relics in Constantinople alleged to be Jesus' authentic burial clothes. In 1080 the Emperor Alexius I Comnenus asked the military assistance of two princes from western Europe, citing the need to defend the relics of Christ kept in Constantinople, which included "the cloths found in the sepulchre following the resurrection."[137] In 1147 King Louis VII of France paid homage to the sacred graveclothes during his visit to Constantinople.[138] In 1157 the Abbot Nicholas Soemundarson returned to Iceland after a pilgrimage to Constantinople and wrote that he had seen, among other things, a "Shroud with the blood and body of Christ on it."[139] Fourteen years later Emperor Manuel I Comnenus showed the relics of Christ's passion, including the Shroud, to the crusader king of Jerusalem.[140]

Of course, there were many relics displayed in cathedrals, churches, and chapels throughout Europe, some of which were perhaps authentic, but most certainly not. Frederick the Wise,

Elector of Saxony (in what is now Germany) in 1520 claimed to own nineteen thousand relics, including four hairs from Mary's head, three pieces of her cloak, four pieces from her girdle, one fragment of Jesus' swaddling clothes, thirteen pieces of Jesus' crib, a piece of gold brought by the Wise Men, one of the nails driven through Jesus' hands, a piece of bread eaten at the Last Supper, and even a twig from Moses' burning bush.[141] The Saxon elector was not to be outdone by his contemporary, the Bishop of Mainz, who claimed to possess *a flame* from the burning bush, along with a feather from the wing of the archangel Gabriel![142] Just because a cloth with the image of a crucified man, purported to be the burial Shroud of Jesus, was prominently displayed in Constantinople for many years does not mean that it was authentic nor does it necessarily link it to the Shroud of Turin.

By 1201 there were in Constantinople a second object that was identified with Jesus' burial. In that year Nicholas Mesarites, who was the overseer of the collection of relics kept in the Chapel of St. Mary of the Lighthouse in the Imperial Palace, successfully discouraged a mob from attacking the palace by reminding them of all the sacred relics that were contained there. Among them were "the *soudarion* [towel, napkin] with the sepulchral cloths, witnesses of the Resurrection. They still smell of perfume, they resist corruption, because they were wrapped around the ineffable corpse [of Jesus]."[143] This *sudarion* was distinct from the sepulchral clothes or Shroud. Ian Wilson theorizes that the *sudarion* was actually a copy of the Mandylion bearing the image of the face only, and that this later became known as "The Veronica," or "Veronica's Veil."[144] The Latin word *veronica*, it is believed, comes from the Greek words *vera ikon,* which mean "true image." This is, however, a matter of speculation.

In the National Szechenyi Library in Budapest, Hungary, there is a book dating to the 1190s known as the *Pray Manuscript*. One of its illustrations has two panels. In the upper panel, Joseph of Arimathea and Nicodemus are shown preparing Jesus' body for burial. The lower panel depicts an angel showing three women the empty tomb of Christ. There are certain features of the portrayal that are reminiscent of the Shroud of Turin. First, the dead body of Christ is depicted without thumbs, although in other illustrations in the book, all five fingers are shown. Second, over the right eye is a bloodstain in the same position as the "3"-shaped stain on the Shroud. Third, in the lower panel is depicted a shroud partly rolled up on the lid of Jesus' tomb. The cloth has a set of little holes that correspond exactly to the four groups of "poker holes" that are not associated with the 1532 fire. Fourth, the shroud in the picture is represented with the herringbone pattern seen on the Shroud.[145]

In 1204, an army of crusaders from western Europe descended on Constantinople, convinced that it was much more convenient and profitable to prey on their fellow Christians there than upon the "infidel" in Egypt and Palestine. Robert de Clari, a French knight, wrote a detailed account of all that he saw in the magnificent city that his countrymen were soon to destroy. Especially impressed by the number of churches and monasteries in Constantinople, Robert doubted that "any man on earth could number all the abbeys of the city." He observed, "It was reckoned that there were in the city a good thirty thousand priests. . . . And if anyone should recount to you the hundredth part of the richness and beauty and the nobility that was found in the abbeys and in the churches and in the palaces and in the city, it would seem like a lie and you would not believe it." Among the wonders he saw at a church called "My Lady Saint Mary of Blachernae," was "the *sydoine* [the translator left the Greek word untranslated into English] in which Our Lord had been wrapped, which [was] stood up straight every Friday so that the features of Our Lord could be plainly seen there." [146]

On April 12, 1204, when the Byzantine emperor failed to hand over to the crusaders a huge sum of money they were attempting to extort from him, the westerners launched a murderous assault on Constantinople, climaxed by three days of massacre, rape, and looting. Robert de Clari noted that after the sack of the city "no one, either Greek or French, ever knew what became of the shroud."[147]

Many people have discounted Robert's account, partly because of the commentary by E.H. McNeal, who translated the work into

English in 1936. McNeal wrote, "Robert seems to have confused *sudarium* (the sweat cloth or napkin, the True Image of St. Veronica) with the *sindon* (the grave cloth in which the body of Jesus was wrapped for entombment). Both relics were in the church of the Blessed Virgin in the Great Palace (Pharos), and not in the church in the palace of Blachernae, as Robert says."[148] However, after reading this commentary, physician and physicist John Heller noted, "I was extremely skeptical that seven hundred years after the event, McNeal could say that an eyewitness: (1) Did not know what he saw and/or misnamed it or (2) Did not know where he was and/or misnamed the place, or (3) Both." He pointed out that *sydoine,* the word Robert used but which was left untranslated, meant "shroud" in medieval French, and that *sudarium* means sweat cloth, and would have been small, too small to have been "stood up straight."[149]

Thus, at the time the crusaders plundered and captured Constantinople in 1204, a relic was housed there that was said to have been the shroud in which Jesus was wrapped, and which seems to fit the description of the Shroud of Turin.

Hardly anyone doubts the existence of the Shroud from the time it was exhibited by the de Charny family who lived in Lirey, a town in northern France, in the 1350s. If this was the same artifact that was displayed for years in Constantinople, what was the status of the relic during the century-and-a-half after Constantinople was sacked?

Some historians have suggested that the Shroud might have been taken and kept by the Knights Templar, an order of soldier-monks. About a century after the Fourth Crusade, the Templars were accused, among other things, of practicing a secret cult to the face of a man with a red beard and red hair.[150] They were disbanded and some of their leaders were imprisoned and eventually killed. In the 1940s at the former headquarters of the Templars in England, a wooden board was found that looked like it had once been the cover of a chest. On the board could be discerned an image of a bearded man that many found to bear a very strong resemblance to the image of the man on the Shroud.[151] How would the Templars have acquired the Shroud? After Byzantine Emperor Isaac II Angelus, who had been blinded and overthrown in a coup several years before the Crusader invasion, was killed in 1204, his widow, the Empress Mary Margaret, married crusader leader Boniface de Montferrat, and the two of them moved to the city of Thessalonica, in what is now Greece. There Mary Margaret founded the Church of the Acheirpoietos, the Image-Not-Made-By-Hands. In 1207 Boniface died and Mary Margaret married Nicholas de Saint-Omer. Their son William was involved with the Knights Templar. Ian Wilson speculated that William de Saint-Omer *may* have given the Shroud, preserved by his mother the ex-empress, to his order.[152]

Other researchers suggest an alternative scenario. There is a letter extant dated August 1, 1205, from Theodore of Epirus to Pope Innocent III, in which Theodore complains that Constantinople was being systematically robbed of her religious relics by the crusaders. He mentions that the Shroud of Jesus had been taken to Athens.[153] In 1207 a man named Nicholas of Otranto, who served as an interpreter, claimed that he had seen the Shroud with his own eyes in Athens.[154] One researcher noted a handwritten document in the City Library of the French city of Besançon, dating to around 1750, which claims that a soldier named Othon de La Roche had sent the Shroud from Greece to his father, Pons de La Roche, in Besançon. Pons, in turn, handed the artifact over to the local bishop, Amadeus of Tramelai.[155] Unfortunately, the archives for the city of Besançon for the thirteenth century have not survived.

There was, in fact, a Shroud of Besançon. It was destroyed by the French revolutionaries in 1794, but paintings of this fabric survive. It was apparently very different from the Shroud of Turin. It evidently displayed a frontal image of a crucified man, but no image of his back. The nail wounds were in the center of the hands. There were no marks of scourging, and, according to one scholar, the body of Christ looked like a stick, straight up and down, with the neck, pelvic area, and knees all of one width.[156] Some have speculated that this Shroud was, in fact, a copy of the true Shroud, which reposed for a short time in Besançon, but which may have been taken to the town of Lirey in the mid-1300s by

Jeanne de Vergy, a member of a prominent local family, when she married the eminent knight Geoffrey I de Charny.

The history of the Shroud during the first thirteen centuries of its putative existence is, of course, informed speculation, which seems reasonable to those who believe in the authenticity of the Shroud, but generally fails to convince those who are skeptical. From the mid-1300s, however, when the cloth was owned by the de Charny family, documentary evidence of the Shroud of Turin is beyond dispute.

Geoffrey (in French, *Geoffroi*) de Charny was a highly respected French knight and nobleman, called by his contemporaries "the most worthy and valiant of them all."[157] Born around 1300, Geoffrey was the son of Jean de Charny, Lord of Lirey, and his wife, Marguerite de Joinville, and had a long and distinguished career, during which he was held for ransom for a short time at Goodrich Castle in Herefordshire in England. He was a devout man who in his *Book of Chivalry* expressed the belief that one achieves success in life only through the help of God and the Virgin Mary. "Men of worth," he insisted, were "those who love, serve, and honor God and His gentle Mother"[158] and who "do not seek to take away the rights of others, but want above all to protect such rights for them and their honor as well."[159] He declared, "No one should have too high an opinion of himself nor should he expect too much praise nor place too much value on it, for the good things and honors of this world are not certain."[160] For Geoffrey, the only certain thing was God, to whom the virtuous were to obtain access through the Virgin Mary. "Pray with all your hearts to the glorious Virgin Mary," he urged, "that with her benign and humble grace and by the holy influence she has over her precious, glorious, and sovereign Lord, Father and Son, that of His noble gentle tender mercy He may . . . look upon your hearts, bodies, and actions, and upon your souls, that He may preserve you, maintain and sustain you in a good state within His holy benign grace."[161]

We do not know how and when this pious and courtly knight obtained the Shroud. Geoffrey's granddaughter later claimed that he had acquired the Shroud as a prize of war. How and when, she did not say. Some *speculate* that Geoffrey *might* have obtained the cloth from the English Templars when he was released from prison in Britain. It is interesting that one of the leaders of the Knights Templar burned at the stake by King Philip IV the Fair in 1314 was named Geoffrey de Charny. One assumes that this Geoffrey was a relative, perhaps an uncle, of the valiant knight, but no genealogical records have come to light to establish nor disprove the connection.

What is clear is that in April 1349, Geoffrey wrote to Pope Clement VI that he was going to build a church in Lirey, France. It was here, at the Church of St. Mary of Lirey, that the Shroud was kept. A letter written three decades later by the Bishop of Troyes declares that around 1355 the Shroud was exhibited to the public. The Cluny Museum of Paris possesses a souvenir medallion from the time[162] which displays the coat of arms of Geoffrey I de Charny and depicts a cloth held by two religious, with a double imprint of the body of a man.

In September 1356, Geoffrey, with the banner of France in his hand, shielding King Jean II with his own body, was killed fighting the English at the Battle of Poitiers. Thirty-three years later, Geoffrey II de Charny, the hero's son and the Shroud's owner, obtained permission from Pierre de Thury Cardinal de Santa Susanna, papal delegate to the court of the French king, for permission to expose "a semblance or representation of the *sudarium* of Our Lord." Geoffrey was able to obtain the approval of King Charles VI, the eccentric king often known as "Charles the Mad," but Pierre d'Arcis, Bishop of Troyes, under whose jurisdiction Lirey fell, but whom Geoffrey had not consulted, was furious. He called a meeting of the clergy in his dioceses and prohibited them from so much as mentioning the Shroud. The clergy of the diocese of Troyes then appealed to Pope Clement VII.

In those days the Church was in a state of "schism" and there were two popes. For many years the headquarters of the papacy had been in Avignon, France, rather than in Rome, but Pope Clement XI had returned to Rome and died there in 1378. However, the papal elections of that year were contested, and as a result, the Italian Urban VI held forth in Rome and claimed the allegiance of England and northern Italy, while the Frenchman Clement VII returned to Avignon, where he was acknowledged as pope not only by France but by Scotland, southern Italy, and Spain. Today Urban VI is considered a legitimate pope and Clement VII an antipope.

However, in 1389, for the Bishop of Troyes as well as Geoffrey II de Charney, Clement VII was pope, and after the appeal of the clergy, the pontiff told d'Arcis to permit the exhibition. The bishop wrote a letter — invariably cited by opponents of the Shroud's authenticity — in which he complained that the canons of the church at Lirey, twelve miles from Troyes, had "falsely and deceitfully, being consumed with the passion of avarice and not from any motive but only of gain, procured for their church a certain cloth cunningly painted, upon which by clever sleight of hand was depicted the twofold image of one man, that is to say the back and front, they falsely declaring and pretending that this was the actual Shroud in which our Saviour Jesus Christ was enfolded in the tomb."[163]

A translator of the document observed that, from his language, the bishop was "not just angry — he was furious, violent, enraged."[164] The prelate continued that the deliberate lie about the origin of the cloth "was put about not only in the kingdom of France, but, so to speak, throughout the world, so that from all parts people came together to view it. And to further attract the multitude so that money might cunningly be wrung from them, pretended miracles were worked, certain men being hired to represent themselves as healed at the moment of the exhibition of the Shroud, which all believed to be the Shroud of Our Lord."[165] Bishop d'Arcis insisted that thirty years earlier (in the 1350s) the cloth had been exhibited, and his predecessor, Henry of Poitiers, making inquiry, had "discovered the fraud and how the said cloth had been cunningly painted, the truth being attested by the artist who had painted it, that it was a work of human skill, and not miraculously wrought or bestowed." Bishop Henry had tried to confiscate this phony Shroud, but the clerics had hidden it. d'Arcis went on to say that "this could not be the real Shroud of Our Lord having the Saviour's likeness thus imprinted upon it, since the holy Gospel made no mention of any such imprint, while if it had been true it was quite unlikely that the holy Evangelists would have omitted to record it."[166]

Geoffrey II also appealed to the pope, and on January 6, 1390, Clement issued a bull, or official letter, stating that (1) the cloth could be exhibited on condition that there were to be neither candles nor incense nor guard of honor, and only with the disclaimer that the cloth was a replica of the Shroud of the Lord, not the real thing, and (2) the Bishop of Troyes was forbidden to oppose the exposition of the cloth, so long as it was carried out in the manner prescribed.[167]

Twenty-eight years later, Margaret de Charny, daughter of Geoffrey II (who had died in 1398) along with her second husband, Count Humbert de Villersexel, made an inventory of their property, and it included "a cloth on which is the figure or representation of the Shroud of Our Lord Jesus Christ, which is in a casket emblazoned with the de Charny crest."[168] Count Humbert promised to give the Shroud to the canons of Lirey, but, after his death in 1438, his widow refused to hand it over, insisting that the cloth was the rightful possession of her family, acquired as a spoil of war. Over the years Margaret held periodic exhibitions of the cloth, and in defiance of the church authorities traded it to Duke Louis I of Savoy and his wife, Anne of Lusignan, in return for a castle and a landed estate. Eventually the ecclesiastical judge of Besançon excommunicated Margaret, who died in 1460.

Between 1453 and 1983, when it was willed to the Vatican by former Italian king Humbert II, the Shroud belonged to the House of Savoy, which reigned as the Italian royal family between 1860 and 1946. Louis I, who regarded the acquisition of the Shroud as his greatest achievement, agreed to pay the priests of St. Mary of Lirey an annual rent as compensation for the loss of the Shroud, a practice abandoned by his son Amadeus.[169] For years the reigning dukes took the Shroud with them wherever they happened to be in their realm. For example, during the 1470s, the Shroud was kept for brief periods at Turin and the nearby towns of Vercelli, Ivrea, Moncalieri, Susa-Avigliano, Rivoli, and Pinerolo in what is now northern Italy, as well as in the Franciscan church at

Chambery, a city in what is now southern France, about one hundred eighty-five miles from Turin, where in a 1483 inventory it was described as "enveloped in a red silk drape, and kept in a case covered with crimson velours, decorated with silver-gilt nails, and locked with a golden key."[170]

In June 1502, Duke Philibert transferred the Shroud from the Franciscan Church to the Royal Chapel of Chambery Castle, where it was placed in a niche behind the high altar, protected by an iron grille with four locks, each of which had a separate key, two of which were held by the duke.[171] On Good Friday of 1503 it was taken by Duke Philibert and his wife to Bourg-en-Bresse, a city about seventy miles north of Chambery, to be shown to Archduke Philip the Handsome of Flanders. At that time, a courtier named Antoine de Lalaing, after describing the ceremonies in which it was displayed to local dignitaries as well as to the public, recounted that in the past a number of tests had been undertaken to ascertain the authenticity of the Shroud. These included burning it by fire, boiling it in oil, and laundering it in a futile attempt to remove the image.[172] He did not go into detail as to the time of the trials or the precise procedure, but if the account is accurate, these trials might well account for the mysterious burn marks that predate the first documented fire that threatened the Shroud.

In 1509 a new reliquary for the Shroud, commissioned by Marguerite of Austria, Duchess of Savoy, was fashioned in silver and placed beneath the High Altar of the Royal Chapel, now known as the Holy Chapel, or *Sainte Chappelle.* In return for her gift of the casket, the dowager duchess required the priests assigned to the chapel to say a daily Mass for her and for the soul of her late husband, Duke Philibert.[173]

Fire broke out in the Holy Chapel during the night of December 3 and 4, 1532, and burning wood embers from the rafters fell on the silver reliquary in which the Shroud was housed. Soon it became so hot that the silver started to melt, and molten drops fell onto and burned through the folded cloth. At this point Canon Philibert Lambert and two Franciscan friars arrived with a blacksmith, who succeeded in opening the casket and removing the Shroud after pouring buckets of water onto the fabric in an attempt to keep it from bursting into flames. The expensive reliquary was ruined, but the cloth was saved, despite the damage done by the water, which blotched the fabric with stains, and the molten silver, which burned a line of holes through the layers of the cloth. The image was largely untouched. Two years later an investigation by three bishops and ten noblemen, all of whom had seen and touched the cloth in the past, was held at Chambery and concluded that the Shroud which then existed was in fact the same Shroud that existed before the fire. The Shroud was then delivered to the Poor Clare convent at Chambery, where the sisters worked for more than two weeks repairing the cloth, patching the burn holes and sewing a backing of Holland cloth to the entire expanse.

The Shroud was housed between 1535 and 1561 first at Nice, in what is now the southeastern corner of France, then at nearby Vercelli, then went back to Chambery again until 1578, when the Archbishop of Milan (and future saint), Charles Borromeo, expressed a desire to see it. To save Borromeo the time and trouble of traveling to France, the Duke of Savoy brought the Shroud to Turin, and kept it there. And in Turin it has remained, housed since 1694 in the Cathedral of St. John the Baptist, except during the years of World War II, when it was removed for safekeeping to a Benedictine monastery in Avellino.

The warlike Pope Julius II, often called *Il Papa Terribile*, or "The Terrible Pope," is best known for commissioning Michelangelo to paint the ceiling of the Sistine Chapel. It was this same Pope Julius who, on April 25, 1506, issued the bull, or official letter, entitled *Romanus Pontifex*, in which he spoke of "that most famous Shroud in which our Saviour was wrapped when He lay in the tomb and which is now honorably and devoutly preserved in a silver casket," and referred to a treatise by his predecessor Sixtus IV, in which the former pope declared that in the Shroud "men may look upon the true blood and the portrait of Jesus Christ Himself." Julius thereupon approved an Office and Mass for the Holy Shroud,[174] with a feast day of May 4. That is as close as the Roman Catholic Church has ever come to declaring that the Shroud is genuine. In 1670, however, the Congregation of Indulgences granted a plenary indulgence to those who made a pilgrimage to see the Shroud "not for venerating the cloth as the true Shroud of Christ, but rather for meditating on the Passion, especially His death and burial."[175]

The faithful, since that time, have had little opportunity to see the celebrated cloth, which was exhibited only eight times during the eighteenth century, mostly to celebrate ducal marriages. It was shown eight times during the nineteenth century. In 1804, while en route to Paris to crown Napoleon, Pius VII, virtually a prisoner of the French dictator, stopped at Turin. He was given a private showing, during which he was seen to kiss the cloth "with tender devotion" in the presence of a number of cardinals and bishops.[176] King Victor Emmanuel I, King of Sardinia, ordered a public exhibition in 1814 to celebrate his restoration after the fall of Napoleon. The next year, Pope Pius VII, returning to Rome after exile by the now-defeated Napoleon, displayed it from the balcony of one of his palaces. The cloth was again shown in 1822, upon the accession to the Sardinian throne of Charles Felix; in 1842, at the marriage of Victor Emmanuel II; in 1868, at the wedding of Prince Humbert (later Humbert I of Italy), when it was displayed for four days at the high altar of the cathedral; and at Turin's Exhibition of Sacred Art in May, 1898.

It was then that lawyer and amateur photographer Secondo Pia (1855-1941) was invited to take pictures of the Shroud. This was a difficult task. There was no electricity in the cathedral. Pia constructed a platform on rails and provided light by means of lamps powered by a portable generator. On May 25, Pia made his first attempt, but a glass filter that masked one of the two lamps broke and he could not proceed. On May 28, at 9:30 at night, Pia tried again. It was 10:45 before the platform was in place and it was 11 when he gave the Shroud a fourteen-minute exposure. This was followed by a second exposure of twenty minutes.[177] Taking the plates home to develop, Pia "nearly jumped out of his skin," almost dropping the plate, when he saw the calm and majestic face emerge in detail on the negative.[178]

After the publication of Pia's photographic prints, two well-respected French scientists, biologist Paul Vignon and Yves

Delage, professor of anatomy at the Sorbonne, published arguments in favor of the authenticity of the Shroud as the actual winding sheet that had enfolded the body of Jesus. However, historian Canon Ulysse Chevalier, another Frenchman, made a study of all historical references to the Shroud or shrouds available to him at the time, and concluded that with the exception of the passage by Robert de Clari (about the Shroud in Constantinople), there is no reference to any body imprint. It was Chevalier who unearthed the fourteenth-century letter by Bishop Pierre d'Arcis that insisted that the Shroud was a fake. The English Jesuit scholar Father Herbert Thurston, in his article on the Shroud in the *Catholic Encyclopedia* in 1913, likewise argued against the authenticity of the Shroud of Turin. He insisted that "it was painted to represent the impression made by the sweat of Christ, i.e. probably in a yellowish tint upon unbleached linen, the marks of the wounds being added in brilliant red." As the image darkened because of the effects of aging and the sixteenth-century fire, "the lights of the original picture would become the shadow of the image as we now see it." Thurston believed that the artist used a living model. As for the anatomical accuracy, the Jesuit argued that "the impressions are only known to us in photographs so reduced, as compared to the original, that the crudenesses, aided by the softening effects of time, entirely disappear."[179] In other words, Thurston was making the argument (no longer tenable after the Shroud was physically studied by scientists) that photography failed to record evidences of human preparation that might be evident if the cloth were studied directly.

The Shroud was exhibited again in 1931 and 1933. During the first of these expositions, it was photographed by the eminent Giuseppe Enrie. It was photographed again in 1969 and 1973 by Giovanni Battista Judica-Cordiglia, and, after another exhibition in 1978, thousands of photographs were made. In 1988, when it was subjected to radiocarbon-dating, it was videotaped.

But until well past the midpoint of the twentieth century, the Shroud of Turin attracted little attention and was regarded by most experts as a work of art rather than an archaeological artifact. Thurston, in his article in the *Catholic Encyclopedia,* stated that "the immense preponderance of opinion among learned Catholics" was that the Shroud was not the genuine winding-sheet of Christ.[180] Peter Rinaldi, a long-time student of the Shroud, recalled than when he was serving as an altar boy at the Turin Cathedral in the 1920s, "I was hardly aware of its presence there."[181] The Shroud, regarded by most as simply a curious relic, began to receive greatly increased international attention after the first serious scientific testing was done in 1973.

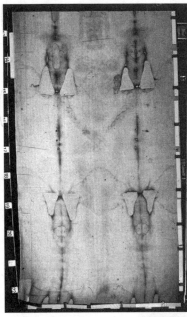

Photos from the Shroud Exhibition in 1973 in Turin. Above, the frontal image; at right, the dorsal image.

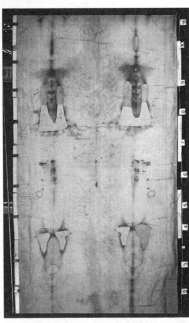

Chapter V

The First
Scientific Tests

By the 1960s there was considerable interest on the part of a number of scientists in making a physical study of the Shroud, but Michele Cardinal Pellegrino, Archbishop of Turin, who was its custodian, proved extremely reluctant to grant permission for such research. Finally in June 1969, the prelate permitted a group of Italian scientists to examine the cloth for two days. The group consisted of eleven members, including an egyptologist, a radiologist, and two forensic experts. They wrote in a report that the Shroud was "in an excellent state of preservation" and suggested that it should be kept between two panes of glass, and that the advisability of the replacement of the current backing should be considered. They recommended further studies:

1. To learn the most probable date of the cloth and patches by means of historical research and physical and chemical tests.
2. To identify the substances present in the image area.
3. To examine the Shroud manually both with and without the backing cloth.[182]

A more complete examination was made in the autumn of 1973 by a team made up of most of the scientists who had made the preliminary study. They included Giorgio Frache, forensic serologist from the University of Modena; Guido Filogamo, director of the Institute of Human Anatomy at the University of Turin; Alberto Zina, another professor from the University of Turin; Enzo DeLorenzi, who headed a radiological laboratory in Turin; Gilbert Raes, a professor of the Ghent Institute of Textile Technology in Belgium; Silvio Curto, a museum curator; Cesare Codegone, a physicist; and Noemi Gabrielli, former curator of the art galleries in Italy's Piedmont region.

This group viewed the Shroud on November 24, 1973, and were allowed to remove seventeen samples, mostly single threads, for study.[183] Three years later, they published their findings in a one hundred twenty page report entitled *La Sindone: Richerche e studi della Commissione di Esperti* ("The Shroud: Research and Studies of the Commission of Experts"). One of the most significant findings was that the body image did not penetrate the cloth, but was confined to the topmost layers of the fabric.

Gilbert Raes, who removed some material from an edge of the Shroud later known as "Raes' Corner," made a microscopic analysis of some of the threads, and concluded that the Shroud had what was known as a "herringbone weave," which in antiquity was generally found in costly materials.[184] Raes also found traces of cotton in the weave, which convinced him that the cloth was woven on a loom also used for weaving cotton. He identified the cotton as a particular type which grows in the Middle East and was not available in Europe before A.D. 800.[185]

Frache studied several threads from the areas of the Shroud that appear to be stained with blood. He subjected them to a test with a chemical solution of benzidine, followed by treatment with hydrogen peroxide. If the threads contained blood, this solution should have turned blue when it came in contact with them. It did not, and Frache and his colleagues therefore had no evidence of the presence of blood on the Shroud.[186] Alan Adler, the American chemist who later demonstrated the presence of blood, believed that his Italian colleagues were unsuccessful because they were unable to get the blood into a solution in order to perform the necessary wet chemical test.[187]

Silvio Curto, the Egyptian museum curator, wrote, "We are inclined to think that it is an artistic impression" from the thirteenth century or later,[188] but admitted that he could find no evidence of paint. Later he would state, "No chemist, no physicist will ever be able to explain how the Shroud image started as a negative or became one at some point in time."[189]

Noemi Gabrielli, the art expert, declared, "If we do not accept the possibility of a miraculous intervention or an unknown photographic process, there are only two possibilities." The first was that the Shroud was a "printed fabric." She conceded, however, that medieval printed fabrics have sharp, clearly defined impressions, and the Shroud image appeared faded "as though the ink had been removed by too many washings or corrosive actions." The other possibility was that the image was "drawn by the artist directly onto a wet cloth stretched on a frame, using a compound of sepia-coloured clay, and yellow ochre diluted in a resinous liquid." The cloth, while still wet, would have been spread over the Shroud and pressed against it with a padded weight. She said that the image appeared to have been transferred onto the cloth "like a drawing on a sheet of paper, but without the material showing evidence of the curves of a body lying underneath, actually wrapped in a cloth, and constantly without presenting distortions on the surface which would appear if a body has been wrapped in it." Her surmise was that the Shroud was "the work of a great artist of the late fifteenth or early sixteenth centuries, who used the Leonardo [da Vinci] technique of shading."[190] (If this were true, it should be pointed out, the image on the Shroud would date to a period a hundred years later than the most recent date that would later be indicated by carbon-dating.)

Max Frei-Sulzer issued an independent report. Professor of criminology at the University of Zurich and a police investigator, he had headed the commission that investigated the plane crash in Africa that killed United Nations Secretary General Dag Hammarksjold in 1961. He was also a botanist and an amateur student of palynology, or the study of pollens. He has been described as a Zwinglian Protestant with little or no interest in religious relics. The Swiss scientist took twelve samples of dust from the Shroud, using a sticky tape that he applied to the surface of the cloth. In that way he was able to pick up "microtraces" without damaging the cloth.

After several years of study, Frei announced that he had found spores from bacteria, mosses, and fungi, as well as plant fibers, fragments of insects, and pollen grains. He identified the pollen of fifty-seven different plants. Twelve were common to France and Italy. Six grew predominantly in Turkey (where Constantinople and Edessa were). Sixteen were Mediterranean plants, found both in southern Europe and the Middle East. Seven grew primarily in Israel and other Middle Eastern countries. The remaining sixteen species were desert plants that grow almost exclusively in Israel. [191] Thus Frei concluded that the Shroud had resided at one time in what is now Israel and also for a time in what is now Turkey, as well as in southern Europe. Answering the anticipated objection that the wind might have carried pollen from the Middle East to Europe, Frei pointed out that ninety-five percent of the pollen of any plant is deposited within a radius of about one hundred meters around it, and the rest reaches "at most a few tens of kilometers." He felt it was impossible for a substantial amount of pollen to be carried twenty-five hundred kilometers in the wind from Palestine to southern Europe.[192] Besides, the transport of pollen in this direction would be counter to the prevailing pattern of winds, which blow from west to east. "The heterogeneous quality and amount of pollen present cannot therefore be explained as a result of accidental contaminations,[193]" Frei contended.

Max Frei died in 1983, before he could publish a final assessment. His studies have been subject to criticism, such as that by J.L. Beaulieu, who in "Critique of the Work of Max Frei-Sulzer," in 1989 pointed out that the Swiss criminologist was an amateur palynologist, "self taught [and] not properly trained." He claimed that Frei's collection was too small and contended that he "claimed an impossible level of accuracy and precision in identifying minute differences in species within genera." Moreover, he worked alone, without consulting any other palynologists. Beaulieu was also suspicious that the pollen on the Shroud was sufficiently well-preserved to permit such confident identification, since pollen grains on a cloth are usually damaged and would have been further harmed by the 1532 fire.[194]

On the other hand, Frei's conclusions were essentially supported by Aharon Horowitz, an Israeli palynologist, and Avinoam Danin, a botanist from the Hebrew University of Jerusalem. Danin wrote that it was possible to demonstrate that the Shroud had at one time been taken through the Negev desert area to the Lebanese highlands.[195] Orville Dahl, who taught palynology both at the University of Pennsylvania and the University of Stockholm (in Sweden), maintained that more than half of the Shroud pollens come from flowers pollinated by insect, and supported Frei in his claim that the pollen on the Shroud — with its origin in the Middle East — could not have been transported to Europe by the wind, because the pollen of flowers does not carry in the air.[196] Frei's collections were eventually obtained by Alan Whanger, professor of psychiatry at Duke University, who dedicated many years to study of the Shroud. He submitted the material for study to microscopists from the Federal Bureau of Investigation, who also generally upheld Frei's conclusions.[197]

Subsequently, researchers have tried to account for the great abundance of flower pollen on the Shroud. Some speculate that at one time the Shroud might have been used as an altar cloth — a linen draped over an altar where Holy Communion was celebrated. Father A.M. Dubarle suggested that the pre-1532 burn holes might have been caused by hot coals dropped from a censor during a liturgical ceremony.[198] Others wonder whether the pollen is a result of mountains of flowers placed in the Shroud along with the victim. This, it has been argued, might be an explanation as to why there is no imprint of the side of the man's face: the flowers were banked up on either side of the body, holding up the cloth and keeping it from draping over the sides of the face and body.[199] In fact, some researchers claim that thirty of the pollens that Frei identified on the Shroud come from flowers which bloom in the spring in Palestine.[200]

The modest study of 1973, which seemed to raise more questions than it answered, aroused new interest in the Shroud on the part of the general public, and other researchers became involved, trying different approaches to explaining the cloth. One of them was Joe Nickell, then a twenty-eight-year-old instructor of English at the University of Kentucky, who had worked as a private investigator and was also a member of the Committee for the Scientific Investigation of the Claims of the Paranormal. He tried to reproduce the Shroud by taking a statue, covering the face with a wet linen, then molding it to the contours of the head, using a powder-puff to apply a light cover of jeweler's rouge, then removing the damp cloth from the face and flattening it. He obtained an image that looked somewhat like that of the Shroud, but much more crude and distorted. There was another difference, too. On the Shroud, the blood-like material has seeped through the cloth, but the image appears only on the surface fibers. However, the image Nickell created with jeweler's rouge did not confine itself to the surface, but permeated the cloth.[201]

Around 1976 the idea of conducting scientific tests on the Shroud caught the attention of Dr. John P. Jackson, a thirty-year-old physicist and Air Force officer who worked at the Weapons Laboratory in Albuquerque, New Mexico. Along with his colleague at the Weapons Lab, Dr. Eric Jumper, an engineer and thermodynamicist who was of the same age, he constructed a full-sized, carefully marked replica of the Shroud so that they could perform experiments in hopes of learning how the curious image was formed. Studying existing photographs of the Shroud, he theorized that if the cloth actually covered a human body, the linen would have had direct contact with certain parts of the body, such as the forehead, nose, and chin, while other areas, like the eye sockets and ears, would have not been touched by the cloth. In collaboration with Bill Mottern, an industrial radiographer at the Sandia Scientific Laboratories of Albuquerque, Jackson and Jumper made use of two devices, the microdensitometer and the VP-8 analyzer, which had recently been used to construct a three-dimensional model of the surface of the planet Mars from photographs transmitted by a satellite. The researchers believed that if the density of the image were measured, and if the image was, in fact, produced by covering a real body, the parts of the body in close contact with the Shroud should appear more dense and those further away should appear more faint.

The microdensitometer measures differences in density in photographs. In a black-and-white photograph the areas that show black are dense with color. The white areas have no color. And in-between areas are many shades of gray. The instrument that the New Mexico scientists were using gives a different number to each shade of color. They analyzed the photographs of the Shroud and fed the resulting numbers into the VP-8 image analyzer, which converted the numbers to vertical relief. In other words, the parts of the body that were close to the cloth should have shown darker than the ones that were farther from the fabric, and so, *if the Shroud had actually covered a real body*, the machine would be able to map its contours. This would not have been the case if the image were painted on.

When Jackson, Jumper, and Mottern ran their tests, they found that the process resulted in a perfect three-dimensional model. It could even be turned sideways so that the face could be seen in profile.[202] When subjected to the microdensitometer and the VP-8 image analyzer, the images created by Nickell did not show the perfect three-dimensionality that the Shroud did.[203] And produced the same sort of distorted reliefs that paintings, drawings, and ordinary photographs generate when subjected to the same process.[204]

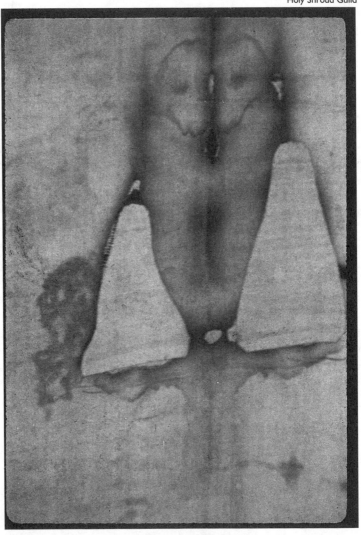

The wound in the side can been seen as a stain at left
(1973 photo).

Chapter VI

STURP and the Tests of 1978

In 1977 Cardinal Pellegrino retired as Archbishop of Turin and "sindonologists," as students of the Shroud are called, hoped that his successor, Anastasio Ballestrero, would prove more amenable to the possibility of scientific testing. Shortly after his installation, the prelate announced that the Shroud would be displayed to the public the following year, to commemorate the four-hundredth anniversary of its acquisition by the House of Savoy.

In March of the same year Jackson, Jumper, Mottern, and other scientists organized the Shroud of Turin Research Project (STURP), which met for the first time in Albuquerque, New Mexico. Father Peter Rinaldi, pastor of Corpus Christi Church in Port Chester, New York, and a well-connected native of Turin (his late uncle had been the head of the influential Salesian Order and a protégé of its celebrated founder, St. Giovanni Bosco), approached the cardinal and told him of the desire on the part of many American scientists to study the Shroud. Ballestrero asked for a written proposal. This was prepared by STURP and accepted by the cardinal. STURP had no official institutional sponsorship and its members had to generate their own funds and perform their research without compensation. Some of the more-than-thirty physicists, chemists, biophysicists, computer specialists, and other scientists who evidently became a part of the group sold cars, took out bank loans, or secured second mortgages. By gift or loan they secured more than two million dollars' worth of scientific equipment.[205]

STURP was headed by a nuclear physicist named Tom D'Muhala. Besides Jackson, Jumper, and Mottern, it included Raymond Rogers, a thermal chemist from the Los Alamos National Scientific Laboratory; Ron London and Roger Morris of the Los Alamos National Scientific Laboratory; Don Lynn of the Jet Propulsion Laboratory of Pasadena; Don Devan of Science, Inc., of Santa Barbara; Roger and Marion Gilbert, from the Oriel Corporation of Connecticut, a husband and wife team who specialized in spectroscopy (which analyzes objects of unknown composition from the wavelengths of radiation they absorb); John Heller, a biophysicist; Ernest H. Brooks, president of the Brooks Institute of Photography; Barrie Schwortz, a photographer from Santa Barbara, trained by Brooks; John D. German and Rudy Dichtl, experts in electric power from the Air Force Weapons Laboratory; and Sam Pellicori, an optical physicist from the Santa Barbara Research Center. STURP has subsequently been criticized for including no experts in textiles, medieval art, medicine, or archaeology.

Some assumed that STURP was comprised solely of committed Christians. David Sox, an American clergyman who taught at the American School in London and authored *The Shroud: Uncovering the Greatest Forgery of All Time*, dismissed the group as "religious fanatics with a military organization."[206] In reality, this was not the case. Peter Rinaldi recalled that within the group there was "a very small number of devout believers, a scattering of agnostics, with a majority of not particularly devout or convinced believers."[207] Biophysicist John Heller was more specific: he counted six agnostics, two Mormons, three Jews, four Roman Catholics, "and an assortment of Methodists, Lutherans, Congregationalists, Episcopalians, and Dutch Reformed."[208] D'Muhala, the coordinator, was quoted as saying, "As far as I was concerned, science was my God."[209] No one was picked by the Church. Alan Adler, who became involved later, recalled that even the members of the team who were religiously devout went out of the way to be impartial when evaluating their data and describing their findings.[210] Not all were convinced of the Shroud's authenticity. Eric Jumper said that (at least initially) he "thought it was totally bizarre that anyone would even fantasize that this might not be a painting."[211]

Between August 27 and October 8, at its home in the Cathedral of St. John Baptist in Turin, approximately three million people viewed the Shroud in its frame of bullet-proof glass. Then, for the next five days, under the supervision of scientific coordinator Luigi Gonnella of the Turin Polytechnic Institute, the American researchers studied the cloth around the clock (with some scientists working while others slept) in the royal palace, which adjoined the Cathedral. There were several European scientists present, including the aging Frei, for whom some of the Americans reportedly showed "scarcely disguised contempt" because of his practice of gathering pollen samples with Scotch tape;[212] Professor Aurelio Ghio from Turin; and Giovanni Riggi, a microanalyst, also from Turin. Heller later wrote, "Everything that was done was logged. Some spectra were recorded on magnetic tape; others were plotted out on X-Y recorders; still more were encoded numerically by hand. Everything was photographed. Everybody was photographed. Every action by every person was photo-recorded so that a complete documentary would be available of each individual's action, location of measurement, and instrumentation. A voice recording was made of every event so that were could be no question of what was done when, by whom, and how."[213]

First of all, the research team, who expected the cloth (even if it was of medieval origin) to be brittle, found it "supple, strong" with the feel of "a new, expensive tablecloth." It had no mildew and was pronounced in splendid condition.[214]

Second, they noted that there were two types of images: the

bloodstains and the body image. The body image, they found (as did the Italian scientists who studied the fabric five years earlier), did not penetrate the cloth, but was confined to the top one or two fibrils. The image was produced by a chemical change in the fibrils resulting from "dehydration, oxidation, and conjugation of cellulose in the fibrils." It appeared that the normal process of decomposition in the linen was somehow accelerated in the image areas.[215]

Ray Rogers, the thermal chemist, was interested in analyzing substances on the cloth to determine how they might have been affected by the fire of 1532. He looked for signs of pigments (either organic or inorganic) such as an artist might have used to paint the Shroud. Under great heat, organic colors run or change colors, and inorganic colors will turn black, or, after they are dried out, run if they are wet. Since portions of the Shroud were drenched in water when it was saved from the fire in Chambery, the water stains were checked for signs of running paints. None were found. Neither did Rogers find evidence of pigments, organic or inorganic.[216]

The researchers looked for signs of protein on the Shroud, since protein would have been used in the binders (in which paint is mixed to bind the colored particles) current in the Middle Ages. Again, the results were negative.[217]

Among the tests performed on the Shroud was "x-ray spectroscopy," by which the team hoped to learn what chemical elements were present on the Shroud. They found the elements the same all over the cloth except for the part where the heels appear on the image. There they found, between the threads, particles of dirt. This could be seen only under a microscope, so it could not have been done by a medieval artist or forger, because the dirt was invisible to the naked eye.[218]

The Shroud was flooded with ultraviolet light. Some substances react to ultraviolet light and glow. Others do not, because they absorb light. The bloodstains did not glow, but there were haloes around the stains that glowed yellow-green under the ultraviolet light. Since blood absorbs ultraviolet light and serum fluoresces, this test was consistent with the idea that the Shroud had actually wrapped a real corpse. If the cloth was stained by contact with human blood and wounds, it would have been natural for the serum to have penetrated into the linen, unseen by the naked eye, beyond where the red blood stopped, as in the case of the Shroud.[219]

Under low-energy x-rays, the weave pattern of the fabric showed up clearly and individual threads could be discerned. Since iron is denser than linen cloth, if the image were made of a reddish paint containing iron oxide (as the pigments a medieval artist would have used to create the figure on the Shroud are believed to have been) the concentrated iron oxide could be easily seen in the x-rays. There was in fact a high concentration of iron oxide at the edges of the water stains, but not in the image,[220] as there would have been had the figure been painted.

The x-ray fluorescence test was also capable of detecting substances like iron oxide and mercury sulfide, which were used in medieval paints. This test showed no traces of mercury. (MgS was identified only occasionally on some sticky tapes by means of microscopy and chemical testing, but was not evident in either of the two x-ray studies.) There was a good deal of iron found on the Shroud. Had the image been painted, there would have been much more on the image of the crucified man than in the area where there was no image. But the iron was evenly distributed throughout the fabric — except in the areas that appeared to be stained with clotted blood. Since hemoglobin in blood contains iron, this test also supported the idea that the cloth once enshrouded a real, wounded body.[221]

The Shroud was studied under low magnification. When magnified thirty to forty times, the image, which appears reddish to the naked eye, appears straw yellow. The yellow was only on the tops of the thread and never on the parts of the threads covered by the weave, which were clean and white. Each thread is composed of about one hundred fibers, each half the thickness of a human hair. The color was only one-to-two fibers deep. Where the image was darker, this was not because the fibers there were colored a darker yellow, but because there were a greater number of colored fibers per unit area.[222] In an interview shortly before his death in 1995, Heller affirmed that the image "does not penetrate beyond the top surface of the thread. In order to paint just a tiny fibril — I liken them to the hair on your arm — those microfibrils — you'd have to have a micro-manipulator, and a microscope with an enormous focal length, so you could see from a distance, and paint each hair individually, and then know how many hairs to paint, so you get a photographic negative, which would develop." On these grounds he personally asserted. "It's not a forgery."[223]

Even when the Shroud was magnified fifty times, the researchers could find no evidence of solid particles (such as would occur had it been painted). This, too, seemed to demonstrate that it was highly unlikely that the Shroud is a painting. Moreover, it was found that the fibers were not cemented together as would have been the case had they been painted. Again, if paint were present, it would have seeped into the threads. But there was no sign of this phenomenon, which is known as *capillarity*. The yellow color of the fibers was never on the covered portions.[224]

The tests that STURP conducted in the fall of 1978 did not prove what the Shroud was, but they seemed to indicate what it was not: a painting. In its report, STURP stated, "We can conclude for now that the Shroud image is of a real human form of a scourged, crucified man. It is not the product of an artist. . . . [The] image is an ongoing mystery and until further chemical studies are made, the problem remains unsolved."[225]

At a press conference in 1981 in New London, Connecticut, where the team presented a detailed report on their studies, someone asked the inevitable question: Had the researchers proved that the Shroud was in fact the burial cloth of Jesus? Ray Rogers, the thermal chemist, rose and said, "In science, you're entitled to any hypothesis you choose, including the one that the Shroud was made by elves from the Black Forest. But you don't have a test for Jesus Christ. So we can't hypothesize or test for that question."[226] When someone, addressing the three dozen scientists on the stage, asked, "All who believe this is the authentic Shroud of Christ, raise your hands," no one did. When a show of hands was requested from those "who don't believe it's authentic," again, no one responded. Finally, when the group was asked, "Have you found anything that would preclude the Shroud's being authentic?" the entire group answered, "No."[227]

Chapter VII

McCrone 'Proves' the Shroud Was Painted

STURP took samples of the Shroud's topmost fibers using small strips of Mylar tape which were pressed tightly against various portions of the cloth.[228] Every part of the Shroud and every type of image was represented.[229] Raymond Rogers proposed that these be sent to the eminent microanalyst Walter Cox McCrone.

McCrone did his undergraduate work and earned his Ph.D. at Cornell University. His very long entry in the 1997 edition of *Who's Who in America* claims that, among his many achievements, he "proved" that the Shroud of Turin is a painting. He was sixty-two years old in 1978, the founder and director of his own research company in Chicago, Walter McCrone Associates. He edited the multi-volume *The Particle Atlas*, which dealt with substances as they appear under the microscope. A few years earlier he had created a stir by declaring as a modern forgery a map of

Photographic enhancement of the face.

Vinland (the area of America explored by the Vikings) that was alleged to date from the Middle Ages. (Since then further studies on the map have led other experts to question McCrone's conclusion.[230]) Because of his experience in working with historical artifacts, McCrone was invited to work with STURP. He attended the first meeting in Albuquerque in 1977, and there he expressed his belief that the Shroud was a painting. At the time, however, most of the other scientists in attendance agreed with him, and therefore his opinion was not controversial.

McCrone did not accompany the group to Italy, nor did he have, then or ever, physical contact with the Shroud. He received, however, the thirty-two samples of Shroud fibers that STURP had collected and, after studying them, said that the yellow coloring on the cloth was due to age,[231] but that the image was colored with red ochre and vermilion paints. He said he had separated the tapes into two groups: (1) those with pigment on the fibers, and (2) those without. The areas where there was pigment were the areas on the body image and the apparent bloodstains. The blank areas of the Shroud were free of pigment particles.

Elaborating, he contended: (1) the Shroud image was due to artists' pigments, because the only colored substances presented in all image areas (twenty-two tapes) and absent in the other areas (ten tapes) were pigment particles; (2) the pigments on the tapes of the image were hydrated red particles which derived from two artists' pigments, known as red ochre (iron oxide) and vermilion (mercury sulfide); (3) an artist used the two pigments to paint the Shroud: the body image was painted with red ochre, the blood images with red ochre and vermilion.[232] McCrone identified the pigments by means of "polarized light microscopy."[233] Performing a test with what is known as "amido black," he observed blue staining from fibers from the image areas, which, he said, confirmed the presence of protein, which would have been a sign of a paint binder.[234] Such findings, he asserted, "prove that the Shroud is a painting probably executed in the middle fourteenth century."[235] The painter, along with the red ochre and vermilion, also used gelatin as a collagen tempera medium.[236] He said that he also tested for blood with the benzidine test used by Frache in

1973 and a test for fluorescence after treating the fibers with H2SO4, and came up with results that were "completely negative for blood."[237]

McCrone insisted, correctly, that there were many shroud-like paintings in the fourteenth century. To create the Shroud of Turin, the painter, McCrone said, prepared a diluted watercolor paint and used a watercolor brush to apply "successive drops to build the desired intensity" of color. "He studied the New Testament of the Bible and earlier paintings of Christ. He then tried to imagine just how a shroud might look. It would not be a typical portrait based on light and shadow. He must have considered a dark tomb with a cloth in contact with the body. If he then formed the image based on contact points between the Shroud and body he would have darkened the brow, bridge of the nose, mustache, beard, cheekbones, hair, etc. Then, as an artist, he would shade the image intensities aesthetically into non-contact areas. In doing so, he, in effect, assigns image density values equivalent to cloth/body distance. This would explain the appearance of the Shroud image, and, as well, STURP's 3-D image construction. Even more important, a photographic negative of such a painted image would automatically appear to be a true positive image."[238]

Art historians have almost unanimously challenged McCrone's claim that there were many paintings in the fourteenth century that were similar to the Shroud. There were, in fact, reproductions of the Shroud itself, but to most art experts, those which have been described or reproduced all seemed to look like ordinary paintings. However, it was common that, after a copy of the Shroud was executed, the artist would touch the fabric of the original Shroud with the reproduction, as a sort of blessing. This would easily account for the small amount of artists' pigments, such as vermilion, that were found on the cloth.[239]

Members of STURP were angered because there had been an agreement that no articles would be published until all findings could be discussed.[240] They were also concerned because McCrone's findings were not consistent with their own. Ian Wilson wrote that "variation in iron content could not be correlated to any of the variations seen in the Shroud's body image coloration. Exactly the same deduction was evident from the absence of any observation of body and blood image in the Shroud x-radiographs. Since whenever quantities of iron oxide sufficient to be visible to the human eye are daubed onto a piece of cloth, they show up under [x-ray fluoroscopy], . . . the only reasonable inference is that whatever is responsible for the Shroud body and blood images cannot be iron oxide."[241]

McCrone was present when STURP met in California at the Brooks Institute of Photography at Santa Barbara. When he announced that the body images had been made by red iron-oxide earth pigments, Pellicori found that he could not believe him. "I've measured the spectrum of iron oxide dozens of times," he said to a colleague. "The color's totally wrong for what he's claiming. Based on spectrophotometry and the x-ray fluorescence findings, there's no way that the Shroud images are composed of iron oxide. . . . He's wrong."[242]

McCrone continued, arguing that the iron oxide had been applied by a finger, and that the image was a finger painting. (Later he would abandon this idea and insist that the iron oxide was suspended in a water solution of animal gelatin.[243]) He said he had observed "snow-fencing," where the iron oxide had piled up on one side of the fibers. He finished by saying that the "blood" on the image was also made up of iron-oxide paint. Heller later wrote, "Slide after slide was projected on the screen, with McCrone pointing out red spots on the fibers, and stating that they were typical red iron earth pigments. I was bewildered. Here was a particle expert claiming that a) the images were the result of iron-oxide red paint and that b) the 'blood' was iron oxide, too. This was completely at odds with the data presented by the x-ray fluorescence team, who saw no increase of iron signal between image and non-image areas, but only where there was blood. It was at variance with what Don Lynn had found in his image analysis, as well as the Gilberts' analysis that the images had a spectrum similar to the light scorch areas. It also left the 3-D aspect of the images unaccounted for."[244]

Asked why he was sure that the red dots he observed were iron oxide, McCrone replied, "Experience." Asked if he had treated them chemically, his answer was, "I didn't have to." When asked to reconcile his findings with the other studies, McCrone simply said, "They must be wrong." To a query as to how his iron-oxide paint theory reconciled with the negative image and the 3-D information, he answered, "Oh, any competent artist could have done that." When one of his colleagues exclaimed, "Do you mean you just looked through your microscope and, without doing specific tests for iron oxide, can proclaim it a painting?" McCrone confidently replied, "Yes."

After that McCrone walked out of the meeting and never again attempted to defend his findings — on which he continuously insisted — before the STURP team. Most scientists publish their findings in journals that have review boards that are fully knowledgeable about the subject, but McCrone published only in his own journal, *The Microscope*. In it he wrote several years later, "I have been unsuccessful in my attempts to convince the STURP scientists of the above facts. I attributed this (and still do) to their lack of background in microscopy, small particle identification, pigments, and paintings. I have spent the last fifty years in just those areas. I expected the scientific world to accept my conclusions. Instead, no one has volunteered to agree with me and most writers have either ignored or contradicted my findings."[245] After "seven years of 'turning the other cheek,' " he complained, "I am now willing to trade 'an eye for an eye'. . . because I see no sign of acceptance of the fact that the Shroud is a painting." Noting that at least thirty other scientists had disputed his conclusions, he went on to offer that "the complete rejection of my work and my conclusions is bewildering and increasingly frustrating." The only way he could account for its rejection was this: "As a few of the more influential of the group [of scientists] decided . . . that the Shroud had to be real, the others followed blindly — a form of mob psychology. They closed ranks and assured the world that I am wrong and the Shroud is real."[246]

Even scientists who do not believe in the Shroud's authenticity dispute McCrone's findings. One writer asserted, "The difficulty with McCrone's theories is that none of the scientists with access to the samples from the Shroud itself has been able to confirm McCrone's findings by experimentation."[247]

In 1996, McCrone, now an octogenarian, privately published *Judgment Day for the Turin Shroud*, in which he forcefully reiterated his belief that the Shroud is a painting and that the cloth contains no real bloodstains. Calling the members of STURP "pseudoscientists,"[248] he accused them of "bad research" and "in certain cases, deceit."[249] He attacked the research of the long-dead Frei by quoting the curious reasoning of Steven Shafersman, a professor of geology at Miami University of Oxford, Ohio. Shafersman insisted that the Swiss scientist's pollen data "can be most reasonably explained by human fraud because the only other possible explanations are that the Shroud of Turin is authentic, that a miracle occurred, or both. Since we are pretty certain that the Shroud is not authentic and that miracles don't occur, human deception is the only explanation remaining."[250]

McCrone went on to say that Rinaldi, also by then deceased, "was convinced the 'Shroud' is a painting but . . . held out against all of my arguments because of his feeling that 'the simple faith of many good people may be somewhat shaken by this turn of events.' "[251] McCrone even insisted that it was partly because of opposition to his work on the Shroud with the polarized light microscope that the subject of "microscopy was rapidly dropped from college studies and from analytical laboratories worldwide."[252]

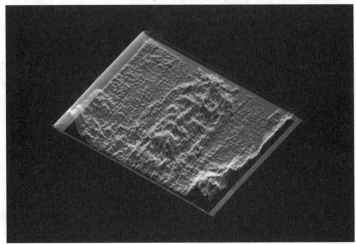

3-D enhancement of the face by the VP-8 Analyzer.

Chapter VIII

Heller and Adler Refute McCrone

In the meantime Pierluigi Baima Bollone, Professor of Legal Medicine at the University of Turin, did two immunological tests on samples from the Shroud, and was convinced that they showed human blood. His work was confirmed a little later by that of two American scientists.

The tapes that McCrone had studied were turned over to two members of STURP, John Heller and Alan Adler. Heller, who was then in his late fifties, had earned a doctorate in medicine from Case Western Reserve and had taught internal medicine and medical physics at Yale before founding the New England Institute for Research in Biophysics and Chemistry. Alan D. Adler, who had recently joined the team, was then in his late forties and had earned his doctorate from the University of Pennsylvania and was currently Professor of Chemistry at Western Connecticut State University.

When shortly before his death Heller was asked in an interview how he had become interested in the Shroud, he answered,

"It's a mystery. It's an unanswered question that should lend itself to scientific verification."[253] Before studying the Shroud and testing it, he was of the opinion that "relics are nothing but flummery from the Dark Ages,"[254] and was convinced that "the probability that the Shroud was a painting was overwhelming." He wrote, "Recent and not so recent discoveries have persuaded me never to sell ancient technology short. Man has an IQ that is no higher today than it was fifty thousand years ago. . . . Periodically, archaeology turns up an ancient artifact that is a real shocker and demonstrates that someone in the distant past was clever enough to figure out something we thought had evolved only in fairly recent times."[255] Adler, who was from a Jewish background, had worked with Heller on various projects in the past, and has been characterized as "a Renaissance man, with an encyclopedic knowledge of the physical and biological sciences, military history, ecology, and many other fields." However, when Heller first approached him, he had never heard of the Shroud of Turin. "The what of where?" he asked when his colleague first mentioned the cloth that he was studying.[256]

After extensive testing, the two scientists were both convinced of the presence of whole blood on the Shroud. They found iron oxide, but its presence was a result of the way that the linen cloth was made and also a consequence of the 1532 fire. Heller and Adler found iron oxide, not on the body image, where McCrone said he saw it, but, in Heller's words, "in a very sharply delineated area of the Shroud and had nothing at all to do with image and body."[257] He accounted for the presence of the iron oxide in the following way: during the fire in Chambery, the water that was poured on the Shroud "reached very high temperatures and, spreading out, had carried with it iron ions bound to the cellulose of the fibers to the edges of the water stains. There, the iron ions had precipitated as iron hydroxide, and dehydration had converted it to iron oxide," which was, in fact, found where the margins of the stain intersected with the image and other features.[258]

Had paint been used on the Shroud, Heller contended, the fibers would have stuck to one another and matted together. The same thing would have happened with "an oily vehicle." Nothing of the sort was seen on the Shroud image, except on the bloodstains, which *did* show the matting and capillarity that would be visible in real blood, which is a mixture of water, cells, and blood proteins."[259]

Heller and Adler found it significant that particles of iron oxide were found within the structure of the fibers. When they looked at the fibers under the microscope, the fibers looked like hollow bamboo stalks with iron "cannonballs" somehow caught within the tubes.[260] No artist, they were certain, could have placed them there. In ancient times, in order to make linen cloth, flax was soaked in water for a long period of time. This process was known as "retting." In this process two minerals, calcium and iron, are attracted to the basic material of the flax, which is cellulose. This demonstrated to Adler and Heller why the x-rays taken of the Shroud showed calcium and iron scattered evenly all over the it. Furthermore, when water was poured onto the Shroud in the fire, some of the iron that was attached to the flax migrated to the edges of the water stains and formed iron oxide. In this process, the red iron-oxide particles were soaked into the cloth. According to Adler, McCrone probably misinterpreted the high concentration of iron oxide in the water-stain margin as red iron-based paint on the image.[261]

Adler and Heller saw vermilion (which was a pigment used in painting) only once, and felt that it was easily explained. "We know that there were artists who painted reproductions of the Shroud; we discovered . . . that very frequently these artists sanctified their paintings by pressing them up against the original. And so we wouldn't be surprised to find occasionally the artist's pigments on the Shroud."

In a 1993 interview Adler recounted, "We pointed out that, yes, we saw what [McCrone] claimed he saw. We saw iron oxide, we saw one piece of vermilion, we saw protein. We also saw red particles that weren't iron oxide. . . . The red we saw was blood, and it was in the blood tape samples from Turin; the only places we saw iron oxide was in the water stain areas and the blood scorch areas. And our explanation is, when you burn blood you get iron oxide — it contains iron."

Continuing, Adler said, "We gave a mechanism why the iron should be expected to be found in the water stain areas. [It was] because the iron is bound to this type of retted linen, and water from dousing the fire formed iron oxide by a series of simple reactions — and we tested it by experiment, and found it was the only way to explain the presence of some iron oxide particles inside the lumen of the fibers."[262]

The x-ray results, Adler indicated, made it clear "that in fact the blood [on the image] can't be composed of mercuric sulfide," because "the mercury stands out. You can't 'see' the blood in the x-rays. If the blood were one third cinnabar like McCrone claims, the mercury would show up on the x-rays, and it doesn't."

As for McCrone's contention that the presence of proteins indicated the presence of a gelatin with which an artist painted, Adler explained, "We ran some very sensitive tests for proteins — and we found out that we could not detect any protein in the image area. The only place we could detect protein was in the blood areas. McCrone claims it's in the image areas, on the basis of microscopic observation — and so it's not up to us to answer him. It's up to him to answer us. We simply asked and tested more questions than he did."[263]

Heller and Adler performed other tests, and confirmed the conclusions of earlier researchers that the images resulted from a straw-yellow color on the crowns of the threads. The absence of capillary action in the image ruled out the possibility that the stain was caused by a liquid or by vapors. As in the earlier examinations, they found that there was no obvious difference in the shade of yellow on the cloth. The intensity of the images was determined by the number of the colored fibrils per unit area. They also found that "whenever one fiber crossed another, the yellow was cut off, and the fiber beneath was white." In addition, they discovered that in most bloodstained areas, the blood had worn off the crowns of the threads and had fallen into the small spaces of the weaving.[264]

Because all known organic dyes and stains can be extracted by a solvent, Heller and Adler tried all kinds of solvents, but could not change the color on the fibrils of the Shroud. The body image could be lightened only by the use of the strongest bleach. This too seemed to preclude the use of paint.[265] Moreover, they could find no trace of aloes, myrrh, or any other spice possibly used at burial, which some scientists believed responsible for the image.[266]

What, then, was the cause of the image? Adler and Heller were aware of the experiments of Jackson and Jumper. We will recall that these scientists had obtained faithful and accurate images from *photographs* of the Shroud, and then engaged police artists to create a faithful *reproduction* of the Shroud, using the three-dimensional images that had been made by the VP-8 image analyzer from the photographs. When the images were subjected to the VP-8 image analyzer, they were all distorted. Jackson and Jumper then took a life-sized bust of a bearded man, and put a photograph of the bust in the VP-8 image analyzer. Again the image was misshapen and deformed. Heller reported, "They tried to do experiments to encode brightness and dimness and authentic distance dimensions." They experimented with hot statues, block prints, engravings, and bas-relief transfers, only to produce "seriously deformed images." They even tried a living volunteer. When they heated a bas-relief, they found that when it was hot enough to cause the areas of the sculpture not in direct contact with the sheet to appear on the linen, the areas that touched the cloth were burnt through.[267]

John Heller and Alan Adler were now convinced that the Shroud was not the product of human skill. Heller wrote that there was "no apparent or even remote chemical mechanism produced by a body with and without anointing oil that could explain the image formation." Moreover, they were convinced that, "There must have been a crucified man inside the Shroud."[268]

After completing over a thousand chemical tests, Adler and Heller published "A Chemical Investigation of the Shroud" in the *Journal of the Canadian Society of Forensic Sciences* in September, 1981. The Society invited them, along with John Jackson, the physicist, and Robert Bucklin, the medical examiner, to debate McCrone in Hamilton, Ontario. McCrone, however, failed to show up, and sent an assistant, who simply quoted his mentor's papers.[269] At a meeting of STURP later that year in New London,

Connecticut, to which McCrone was invited but which he refused to attend, Adler, when questioned about how he could answer McCrone's contention that the apparent blood was simply a mixture of red ocher and vermilion, presented a list of tests that confirmed the presence of blood on the Shroud: "(1) High iron in blood areas by x-ray fluorescence; (2) Indicative reflection spectra; (3) Indicative microspectrophotometric transmission spectra; (4) Chemical generation of characteristic porphyrin fluorescence; (5) Positive hemochromogen tests; (6) Positive cyanomethemoglobin tests; (7) Positive detection of bile pigments; (8) Positive demonstration of protein; (9) Positive indication of albumin; (10) Protease tests, leaving no residue; (11) Positive immunological test for human albumin; (12) Microscopic appearance as compared with appropriate controls; (13) Forensic judgment of the appearance of the various wound and blood marks."[270]

Adler later said, however, that he and Heller were not willing to declare that the blood was beyond the slightest doubt human blood. "We were willing to say it was a primate's blood," he affirmed, adding, "If you choose to think that the image you see is that of a chimp or an orangutan, you're perfectly welcome to believe that."[271]

Some researchers have questioned why the blood on the Shroud appears so red, when ancient dried blood usually appears black. Adler had an answer for that: the blood that is seen in mummies (for example) looks black because there is a thick layer of blood. However, "If you look at a thin section of it, you'd see it was brown." However, the *red* hue of the blood on the Shroud is due to a different factor. On the Shroud, he explained, "there is a very high amount of one of the blood break-down products, bilirubin. When a person is severely injured or subject to great trauma, red blood cells are broken. The hemoglobin goes through the liver, and what the liver does is to take the broken blood cells . . . and converts it to what are called bile pigments: biliverdin and eventually bilirubin for excretion." Adler explained, "The reason why the blood is red is that when it clots, as in the case of . . . a wound here, you see around the edge of the wound there is serum, squeezed out around it. The clot contracts because of the fibrin in it. And it squeezes out the serum. The serum, the exudate [that is, what is given off or squeezed out], has excess albumin in it, and has a small amount of hemoglobin, and the albumin carries all the bilirubin that's there. . . . So what you've got on the exudate of the clot is in fact a blood-derived protein mixture when you've increased the ratio of bilirubin to hemoglobin, over what you'd see in normal blood. And the spectrum of the hemoglobin changes to give you a sort of reddish-brown color, the brown color, that happens to oxidized blood — you're right, when blood ages this color change takes place. But bilirubin is yellow-orange. Especially when it's bound on the protein. And if you mix the two, what do you get? You get red. And so the fact that the blood is red, and still red, is proof of the fact that this is blood from a man who died a very traumatic death. Which is in agreement with the pathological image evidence."[272]

Nearly everyone who studied the findings of Heller and Adler agreed with them that the red stains on the Shroud of Turin are the blood of a primate, and that the image was not painted nor produced in any other way by any known form of human endeavor. One vocal exception remained, of course: Walter McCrone, who called the findings of Heller and Adler "asinine" and publicly declared, "Adler is an ass."[273]

In the following years, more studies were made of the blood on the Shroud. Gilbert Lavoie, an American physician, demonstrated in 1983 that he could successfully transfer images of blood clots very similar to those on the Shroud onto cloth, provided that no more than two-and-a-half hours elapsed between the cessation of the blood flow and the contact of the clot with the cloth.[274] Moreover, he was convinced that "the blood marks [on the Shroud] were made by a contact process" but that "the image was not made by a contact process."[275] In other words, the blood marks and the image were formed by two completely different processes and also at different times.[276]

In the early 1990s Dr. Victor Tryon, director of the Center for Advanced DNA Technologies at the Texas University Health Science Center, obtained from Italian scientist Giovanni Riggi some small samples that Riggi had taken in 1988 from the area of the Shroud's crown of thorns on the day that he also had removed material from "Rae's corner" for radiocarbon-testing. Dr. Tryon and his wife Nancy, who was his chief technician, on examination of a 1.5 millimeter fragment on sticky tape, were able to confirm that it was blood from a male human being and were also able to "detect pieces of double-stranded DNA" and found "three quite unmistakable gene segments."[277]

Then in 1995, scientists from the Genoa Institute of Legal Medicine were able to examine two threads that were 1.5 centimeters in length that had been taken from the foot region of the Shroud by Italian scientists when they worked with the STURP team in 1978. Professor Marcello Canale reported that they had been able to extract DNA from the threads.[278]

The fact that it does in fact contain bloodstains does not, however, reveal the owner of the blood nor the time or manner that it was deposited on the Shroud.

Chapter IX

Coins, Flowers, and Icons

Scientists found other interesting features connected with the Shroud. Joseph Kohlbeck, an optical crystallographer working for the Hercules Aerospace Divisions, which makes missiles, found particles of aragonite with small amounts of strontium and iron on the Shroud's fibers on the image of the foot. With the help of archaeologist Eugenia Nitowski, he obtained samples of limestone from inside ancient tombs in and near Jerusalem and subjected them also to microscopic analysis. He found the same substance. The aragonite on the Shroud and in the tombs was an uncommon variety, deposited from springs, typically found in limestone caves in Palestine, but not in Europe. The samples from the Shroud and the tombs provided "an usually close match," suggesting to him and to Nitowski that the Shroud had once been in one of the "rolling-stone tombs" that were common in Palestine around the time of Christ and for several centuries before. Kohlbeck observed that those who believe that the Shroud is a forgery need to explain how the very rare aragonite found its way to the surface of the Shroud.[279]

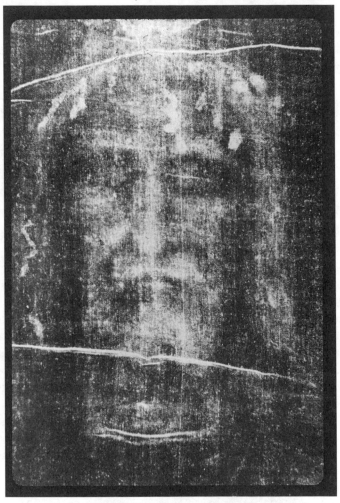

Negative image of the face.

Features even more striking were observed on the Shroud. As we have seen, medical examiner Robert Bucklin noted "rounded foreign objects can be noted on the imprint in the area of the right and left eyes."[280] Jackson and his colleagues also noticed "button-like objects" over each eye in their VP-8 relief.[281] These objects are much more distinct in the 1898 and 1931 photographs than those taken in 1978. It was thought that some of the threads that ran through the eye area on the cloth had been pulled or rotated, perhaps during the 1973 examination.[282]

Giulio Ricci, in his "Historical, Medical, and Physical Study of the Holy Shroud" examined five possible explanations for these objects: (1) "nonuniformity in the image forming process"; (2) the arrangement of the cloth on the man of the Shroud in such a way that it hung close to the eyelids; (3) "a local biological, chemical, or thermal reaction" that occurred some time during the shroud's existence; (4) the result of an artist's attempt to enhance the eyes of the image; or (5) swellings on both eyelids due to physical abuse. He ruled out the first and third possibilities because there were no other three-dimensional irregularities on the entire length of the cloth, which, he said, would make very unlikely the possibility that some image-forming process acted on both eyes of the image but nowhere else on the cloth. He rejected the second possibility, because if the cloth were draped close to the eyelids it would have sagged in the region of the nose and caused the nasal region between the eyes to appear distorted in the relief pictures — and this was not the case. Moreover, Ricci observed that the edges of the "objects" fell off too sharply "to be accounted for by a simple sag in the cloth over the eyes" or be explained by swollen eyelids. Furthermore, he discounted the idea that the objects were painted because "the color and character of the image in the eye regions are indistinguishable from other parts of the Shroud image," which means that the hypothetical artist would have been forced to devise a process similar to that which created the image on the Shroud in the first place. Therefore Ricci insisted that there was but one conclusion possible, and that was "that the button-like features are . . . *solid* objects resting upon the eyelids."[283]

Jackson believed that the button-like objects were in fact coins placed by Jesus' family and friends to keep his eyes closed after death. Research by Francis L. Filas, a professor of theology at Loyola University in Chicago, tended to support this hypothesis. Using high-magnification photography, Filas found the letters UCAI on the right eye, arranged in a coin-like curve. He thought that these might be the central letters of the coin inscription TIBERIOU CAISEROS — Greek for Tiberius Caesar, who was Roman Emperor during the time of Christ's ministry. He also found over the eye a tiny design that looked like a shepherd's crook. He was able to locate authentic Roman coins, minted between A.D. 29 and A.D. 32 (which was the time of Jesus' ministry) that contained a shepherd's staff as well as the Greek inscription TIBERIOU CAISEROS.

Filas died in 1985, but his research was confirmed by Alan and Mary Whanger. We will remember that Whanger was a professor of psychiatry at Duke University, and also an expert in photography, who along with his wife, Mary, between 1979 and 1981 developed the "polarized image overlay technique" in which two images were projected one on top of the other and aligned onto the same screen through polarizing filters at right angles to one another, thereby causing the two images to fade into one another when they were viewed through a third polarizing filter.[284] This made it possible to analyze the features of one image that corresponded to, or were congruent with, those of the other.

Comparing a photograph of the Tiberius Caesar coin, known as a *lepton*, or "widow's mite," with a computer-enhanced photograph of the area over the right eye of the Shroud image, they found "a very close match," noting at least seventy-four "areas of congruence." In other words, the Whangers found seventy-four features on the coin that closely corresponded to features on the Shroud image. They wanted to be sure that they were not simply seeing what they wished or expected to see, so they repeated the overlay comparison, first by reversing the coin from right to left, and then by reversing the top and bottom. When they reversed the sides, they found only ten points of congruence and when they turned the coin upside down they found only six. Then they compared the Shroud image with a lepton of the same size and shape but with a different inscription, and there they found only eleven points of congruence.[285]

The image of the object over the left eye on the Shroud is fainter than that over the right, but the Whangers found seventy-three points of congruence between that image and a Roman coin, contemporary to the time of Christ, known as a "Julia lepton."[286] The Whangers sent their findings to be checked by Robert Haralick of the Spatial Data Analysis Laboratory of the Virginia Polytechnic and State University (Virginia Tech). Haralick gave "cautious support" to the Whangers and to Filas, but noted, "Science has no way of determining whether what appears as a coin inscription is anything but a random quirk of the Shroud's weave."[287] He offered, "The evidence is definitely supporting evidence because there is some degree of match between what one would expect to find if the Shroud did indeed contain a faint image of the Pilate coin and what we can in fact observe in the original and in the digitally processed images."[288] Some have speculated that the apparent inscription might possibly have been produced by the texture of a negative film which, when observed through a microscope, "could appear as a group of silver lines forming alphabetic characters." This argument has been answered, however, by researchers who insist that none of the "presumed alphabetic characters" on the negative can "be proportionally reproduced in an enlargement."[289]

Although at various times and in various places coins have been placed on the eyelids of the dead, some have questioned whether this was actually the custom among the Jews at the time of Christ. Greeks and Romans characteristically placed coins on the eyes of the dead as payment to Charon, who was believed, in folk religion, to guide the souls of the dead across the River Styx. Such a custom would, of course, have been anathema to pious Jews. However, it seems to have been a Jewish custom to close the eyes of the deceased, and the placement of coins was a practical way of keeping the eyelids shut. Archaeologists working in Israel have, in fact, found coins in the eye orbits of three skulls from the approximate time of

Jesus.[290] Although this would certainly not prove that this was a common practice, it would seem to indicate that it was not unknown at the time and place.

Using their polarized image overlay technique, the Whangers have detected still more objects on the Shroud. On the forehead of the man of the Shroud many have made out the shape of a three-sided box at the base of the forehead and a V-shaped marking that extends below it at the bridge of the nose. When Haralick at Virginia Tech examined the Shroud image, he found that this object had "a non-physiological three-dimensional structure." He also detected a band extending around the head (on both front and dorsal images) at the level of this box. The Whangers believed that this box was a "phylactery." Phylacteries were little boxes containing verses of Scripture that devout Jewish men wore on their foreheads and arms. Jesus criticized the Jewish leaders of His day who liked to wear large, wide phylacteries so that people would know how religious they were, but who were nonetheless destitute of inner qualities of genuine spirituality (see Mt 23:5). The image of the little box on the Shroud the Whangers found very similar to a first-century phylactery discovered in one of the caves at Qumran (where the Dead Sea Scrolls were found). They were convinced that when the Shroud victim was killed, someone, apparently to insult him, ripped open the front part of the leather pouch, thereby creating the V-shaped image. The Whangers also found evidence of the phylactery the man wore on his left arm, after noting that the blood flow pattern on the left forearm was quite different from that on the right. It separated into seven streams, and they were convinced that this might have been the result of the presence of a leather strap.[291]

The Whangers have also detected images of many flowers and plants which, they wrote, "closely resemble images that are made by a coronal type of energy discharge." The images they found, faint and of low contrast, are of "partially wilted flowers and plants bunched together, which makes them difficult to perceive without some photographic or computer enhancement, or without a comparative template of some sort." They found images not only of flowers, but buds, stems, and fruit, which they

said they recognized by comparing them with botanical drawings. "We feel we have made tentative identification of twenty-
eight of these plants, which we have photographed in detail. Of
these plants, all twenty-eight grow in Israel; either in Jerusalem
itself or in the nearby desert or Dead Sea areas." Twenty-five of
the plants that they observed were detected by Max Frei in his
pollen study. Most of these bloom in March and April.

The Whangers believed that the flower images were more visible in the early centuries of the Shroud's existence, since they
found these blossoms depicted in many images of Christ that were
executed between the third and tenth centuries.[292]

The Whangers also saw a crucifixion nail, a Roman spear, a
sponge on a stick, a crown of thorns, two scourges, a large ham-
mer, and a pair of pliers.[293] They cited a Jewish custom, which
they believe was observed in the time of Christ, that anything that
came in contact with the lifeblood of the deceased was buried
with him.[294] The presence of such items associated with the man's
torture and death would presuppose the cooperation of his executioners. If one believes, as the Whangers do, that the image on the
Shroud is that of Christ, and if one believes the Gospel account
that a centurion present at the crucifixion of Jesus remarked,
"Truly, this man was the Son of God" (Mt 27:54; Mk 15:39), it is
possible to believe that a sympathetic Roman officer may have
recovered all the items touched by His lifeblood, and turned them
over to His family.

The Whangers also used the overlay technique to compare the
Shroud with portraits of Christ from the early Middle Ages. It is
obvious to anyone who has seen a picture of the man of the Shroud
that he bears a strong resemblance to the stereotypic representation of Jesus: he has long hair, parted in the middle; a long, narrow face; a long, narrow nose; large, luminous eyes; and a beard
and moustache. There are, however, no descriptions of Jesus in
the Scriptures. There are no descriptions of Him in early Christian writings. For example, St. Augustine, bishop of Hippo in North
Africa in the early fifth century, and one of the most important of
the "Church Fathers," wrote that nobody had any idea what Jesus
looked like and that, over the years, His portraits had been "innu-

merable in concept and design." [295] Typically, during the first few centuries after the time of Jesus, He was represented symbolically as a beardless youth, usually either carrying a sheep on His back as "The Good Shepherd," or as the Greek and Roman sun god Apollo, because of His role as the "sun of righteousness" and as the Light of the World. Around the year 400, the portraits of Jesus started to resemble the bearded and majestic image of Jupiter, the king of the Roman gods.

The images that the Whangers analyzed are mostly Byzantine icons. Icons, stylized portraits of Christ, Mary, or the saints, are very important today in the worship of the Eastern Orthodox Church. This branch of Christianity crystallized in what are now Greece, Turkey, and the Middle Eastern countries, in what was then the Eastern Roman Empire, or Byzantine Empire. Thus, the artistic genre of most of the portraits that bear similarities to the Shroud is Byzantine art or iconography. It was in Byzantine art that what is now the conventional portrayal of Jesus first appeared, in the 500s and 600s.

As early as the 1930s, Paul Vignon, who had been studying the Shroud since the turn of the century, observed that in Byzantine portraiture there was a recurrence of unusual features that seemed to derive from the Shroud. These oddities, noted by many others throughout the years, include: l) long hair, parted in two at each side of the face; (2) a short tuft of hair on the forehead; (3) prominent eyebrows; (4) a triangular mark on the bridge of the nose; (5) large, deep, staring eyes; (6) a long, straight nose; (7) pronounced cheekbones; (8) sunken cheeks; (9) a small mouth visible despite the moustache; (10) a beardless area below the lower lips; and (11) a forked beard.[296]

The sixth-century icon portrait of Christ called "The Pantocrator" (ruler of the universe) from St. Catherine's Monastery on Mount Sinai bears a particularly strong resemblance to the Shroud. Professor Kurt Weitzmann of Princeton University, who made no connection with the Shroud, nonetheless noted that "the pupils of the eyes are not at the same level; the eyebrow over Christ's left eye is arched higher than over his right . . . one side of the mustache droops at a slightly different angle from the other, while the beard is combed in the opposite direction." These are all oddities of the Shroud image, and Weitzmann notes that "many of these subtleties" appear in many other portraits of Christ in Byzantine art.[297] When the Whangers compared the Pantocrator icon with the Shroud they found no less than one hundred seventy "points of congruence," [298] leading some students of the Shroud to speculate that the artist who painted the Pantocrator copied the Shroud from life.

The Duke University researchers also studied dozens of Byzantine coins bearing the likeness of Jesus, and found similarities to them as well. In one, a *tremissis* from the reign of Justinian II, they found one hundred forty-five points of congruence.[299] Some of the features from the Shroud that appear on the icons or coins are simply marks or folds on the cloth, but this can be determined only by studying the negative with computer-enhanced photography. The medieval artists, if they copied the Shroud, had to go by only the murky positive image.

Starting about the eleventh century, some Byzantine icons show Jesus with one leg shorter than the other. Even some portrayals of the infant Jesus show a withered and deformed limb.[300] Indeed, some icons of the crucified Christ show a crooked footpiece, fashioned to accommodate limbs of unequal length. Many Shroud researchers are certain that this peculiar artistic convention resulted because the man on the Shroud, when viewed superficially with the naked eye in the positive image, *does* appear to have a short left leg. This is, however, because this leg apparently was fixed to the cross in a more curved position than the right when its owner was crucified and, because of rigor mortis, remained bent in death.

The incorporation of minor details of the Shroud image into many examples of Byzantine art, even those which turn out to be the result of folds or blemishes in the cloth, convinced many people that the stereotypical portrait of Jesus comes from none other than the Shroud. This, and features such as the images of the eye coins and of the banks of flowers, convinced many researchers that the body of Jesus Christ was once enshrouded in the cloth from Turin.

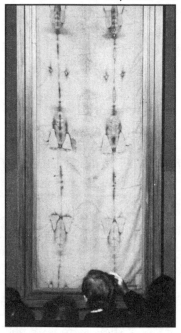

1973 photos of the frontal image (at left) and the dorsal image (below).

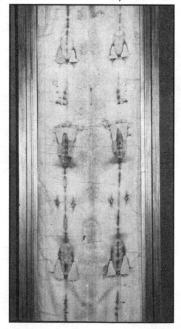

Chapter X

Carbon-Dating the Shroud

Every living thing, animal or plant, absorbs from the atmosphere carbon 12 and its radioactive isotope, carbon 14. When plants and animals die, they no longer ingest new carbon, and the carbon 14 that they already contain begins to change into carbon 12 at a measurable rate. It was in the 1950s that a scientific test was devised to date archaeological artifacts by measuring the rate of the decay of carbon 14.

Although radiocarbon-dating is considered the most accurate way of dating ancient objects, it involves certain difficulties and is not always accurate. In his book *Holy Faces, Sacred Places*, Ian Wilson gives several examples of erroneous dating. In one instance, scientists tested artifacts from the island of Santorini in the Aegean Sea, where a terrible volcanic eruption occurred (according to most historians) around 1500 B.C. Some of the artifacts from the time of the disaster carbon-dated as early as 2590 B.C, plus or minus eighty years, and other artifacts from the time of the eruption carbon-dated 1100 B.C, plus or minus one hundred ninety years. Even if the date of the eruption assumed by historians is inaccurate, the carbon-dating in question was useless in correcting it because it provided a range that covered a period of fourteen hundred years. Wilson cited another instance from 1984, when a well-preserved corpse was found in a peat bog in Cheshire, England, and tested by laboratories in the English cities of Oxford and Harwell. All the Oxford samples carbon-dated to the first century A.D., while all those from Harwell dated, consistently, to the fifth century A.D. Suspecting that the discrepancy in dates must have resulted from different pretreatment procedures used in the two laboratories, Oxford and Harwell swapped samples, but the measurement still came out the same, and no one was able to say for certain (at least at the time when Wilson wrote) why they did.[301]

While some researchers were eager to undertake the carbon-dating of the Shroud, other experts expressed caution. Robert Stuckenrath, a long-time researcher in radiocarbon-dating, wrote, "The date of a sample whose provenance is in doubt is worse than useless — it is misleading."[302] In other words, because so many factors, both apparent and unknown, can skew carbon-dating, testing an object like the Shroud could hardly be done with confidence, since nobody knows for sure where it was throughout the entirety of its history, much less the conditions under which it was preserved or the substances that came in contact with it and thereby "contaminated" it.

William Meacham, archaeologist from the University of Hong Kong, wrote, "There appears to be an unhealthy consensus approaching the level of dogma among both scientific and lay commentators, that C-14 testing will 'settle the issue once and for all time.' This attitude contradicts the general perspective of field archaeologists and geologists, who view possible contamination as a very serious problem in interpreting the results of radiocarbon measurement."[303] He doubted that anyone "with significant experience in the dating of specimens from excavations can forget for a single instant the potential risk of contamination and other sources of error." He went on to say that "no competent archaeologist would trust a single date or a series of dates on just one point to define an important historical reality, to establish a site or a cultural chronology. No radiocarbon scientist can state with certainty that he has removed all the contamination or that a series of dates produced for a specimen are beyond any doubt its effective calendar age. The public and many non-specialist academies seem effectively to share the erroneous concept that carbon 14 dates are absolute. . . . One or two dates should never be used by themselves to establish the chronology of a site. The dates that have revealed themselves to be useless are so numerous, either as a result of contamination or from other causes, that a radiocarbon chronology with such prerequisites of reliability can be determined only if a number of dates regarding the same site re-enter in a homogenous scheme that agrees with the stratigraphic sequence."[304] In other words, dates determined by radiocarbon testing should be considered accurate only if they tally with other tests.

Another problem in subjecting the Shroud to radiocarbon testing was that the "Proportional Counter Method," which was used exclusively until the 1970s, required the destruction of a large area of the cloth. Around 1977, researchers at both the University of Rochester (New York) and the University of Toronto devised a system called accelerator mass spectrometry, or "AMS," that could date very small specimens.

In 1982, Alan Adler took a single thread that had earlier been taken from the Shroud and sent it to the University of California to be carbon-dated at the nuclear accelerator facility there. The results were curious. One end of the thread dated to 200 A.D., the other to A.D. 1000. In an interview many years later Adler conceded, "The test was not performed under rigorous conditions; the dates were not corrected by the dendrochronological curve; we do not even known which end . . . gave the earlier date; the experimenter was not experienced in C-14 testing. The results of that 1982 tests should be thrown out."[305]

In 1985, archaeologist Meacham proposed testing five samples from the Shroud: (1) a single thread from the middle of the cloth, between the dorsal and ventral images; (2) a small piece cut from the edge next to the site where textile specialist Gilbert Raes took his sample in 1973; (3) a piece of charred cloth; (4) a piece cut from the side strip next to the place where Raes had cut; and (5) a piece of cloth sewn on in 1534 to repair damage from the fire that had occurred two years earlier. All of these samples would be subjected to elaborate pretreatment, electronic microscopic selection, and testing for impurities and "intrusive substances" such as "higher order hydrocarbons, [and] inorganic and organic carbonates." Samples number two and five would be measured by both of the methods in use to measure carbon 14.

The following year Meacham and about a dozen others, including seven radiocarbon-dating specialists, three scientists from STURP, and a representative of the pope, met and proposed a "protocol," or a plan, for testing the Shroud. It was agreed that seven different labs would be involved, some using the proportional counter method and others making use of the newer AMS method. They now proposed to date seven samples, taken from seven different sites on the Shroud, none of which had been burnt by the fire.[306]

The Vatican, the owner of the cloth since the death in 1983 of former King Humbert II of Italy, gave permission for the testing of the Shroud. In charge were the archbishop of Turin, Cardinal Ballestrero; his scientific advisor, Luigi Gonnella, whose scientific expertise was in metrology, or measurements; and Gonnella's assistant, Giovanni Riggi, a microanalyist who specialized in the conservation of museum artifacts. To the horror of nearly all those who had submitted the protocol of 1986, Gonnella and Riggi twice simplified the procedure so that their plan was to test only one sample, which would, in turn, be cut into three pieces and tested by three laboratories, all of which used the AMS method of dating. Even Harry Gove, who helped to develop the AMS procedure and who tended to be very critical of STURP, was outraged. Along with Garman Harbottle, who developed the proportional counter method of testing, he wrote the pope, declaring that Gonnella and Riggi were making a grave mistake if they approved "a limited or reduced version of the research, whose outcome will be, to say the least, questionable." Using only one sample, if there were some reason that the carbon 14 content in it was somehow contaminated, it would be rendered inaccurate, and "it would give the same answer to all three labs, and all three would be wrong."[307] Harbottle warned that in following the Gonnella-Riggi protocol, "we are opening the door, perhaps, to an enormous controversy, to endless disputes and recriminations that could stretch on forever."[308]

On April 21, 1988, under the supervision of Gonnella, representing the Pontifical Academy of Sciences, and Michael Tite, a British scientist who was to coordinate the work of the three labs, a sample was cut from the section of the Shroud where Gilbert Raes had made his cuttings. Meacham had warned against taking the sample here. Because it was near a water stain and because the area had been patched and cut, there were enough unanswered questions about the condition of the cloth in that region that he insisted the specimens taken from it should not be considered as typical of the Shroud as a whole.[309] "Raes' Corner" was generally considered the most contaminated part of the cloth. It was believed that this was the area from which the Shroud had been held or suspended in public exhibitions in the past. When asked why they selected their sample from that site, Gonnella and Riggi simply said, "Because that is where it had been cut before."[310]

The samples, which were about the size of a postage stamp, were cleaned. Some of the scientists who had proposed the original protocol were concerned because no chemist was present to supervise the process.[311] The samples were then hand-delivered to laboratories at the University of Arizona at Tucson, Oxford University, and the Swiss Federal Institute of Technology in Zurich. These labs were also given pieces of other cloths, for which the dates were known. None of the pieces was labeled, so that the researchers performing the tests were not supposed to know which of the four pieces came from the Shroud. However, the pattern of weaving characteristic of the Shroud was so well-known that despite the absence of labels, it was not difficult to identify the fragment as from the Shroud. Once each lab completed its work, the results were to be sent to Michael Tite at the British Museum. No information was to be given out to the public until the work of all three was complete and the conclusions were in the hands of Cardinal Ballestrero.

Despite the promise of confidentiality, on July 3, 1988, London's *The Sunday Telegraph* ran a story in which it claimed to have "intercepted signals" telling that as a result of the tests the flax of the Shroud had been shown to be of medieval origin. Then, on August 26, *The Evening Standard* ran a story with banner headlines, proclaiming the Shroud a fake, dating from about 1350.[312]

Both Tite and Ballestrero refused to comment until a news conference was called in the fall of that year. On October 13, Cardinal Ballestrero met with the press at the Salesian Mother House in Turin and read a carefully worded statement which began: "With a dispatch delivered to the Pontifical Custodian of the Holy Shroud on September 28, 1988, through Dr. Tite of the British Museum, the coordinator of the project, the laboratories at the University of Arizona, Oxford University, and Zurich Polytechnic, which carried out the radiocarbon measurements of the fabric of the Holy Shroud, have finally communicated the results of their operations."[313] A sample of cloth from Nubia had accurately tested as originating between A.D. 1026 and 1160. A fragment from Thebes, in Egypt, had revealed a date between 9 B.C. and A.D. 78, which was its proper age. A piece of cloth from medieval France showed a date of origin between A.D. 1263 and 1283. As for the Shroud, "the interval of calibrated dates assigned to the fabric of the Shroud, with a degree of certainly of 95 percent, lies between 1260 and 1390 A.D." Ballestrero, protesting charges made by various newspapers that the Church was withholding the results because the information made it look bad and because it was "afraid of science," went on to say, "While submitting to science the evaluation of these results, the Church confirms its respect and veneration for this venerable icon of Christ, which remains a cult object for the faithful in accordance with the attitude that has always been demonstrated towards the Holy Shroud, in which the value of the image is pre-eminent with respect to its possible value as a historical object."[314]

Gleefully, newspaper editors all over the world screamed in their headlines that the most venerable "relic" of the Roman Catholic Church had been *proved* a medieval fraud. A friend met Peter Rinaldi, and told him, "I feel terribly sorry for the Church and for you." Rinaldi replied, "You can't be serious. Do you really think the Church will fall apart because the Shroud may not be what many of us supposed it to be? The Church has nothing to fear from truth, provided, of course, it is backed by solid facts."[315]

Nearly all those involved in the testing of the fabric were satisfied that the Shroud was medieval. Tite commented, "I have no more interest in the Shroud, now that the odds are astronomical against [it] dating from around the time of Christ."[316] Edward Hall, director of the Oxford laboratory, said somewhat ungraciously, "No one of any scientific worth [can] now believe otherwise than that the Shroud is a fake. Anyone who [thinks] otherwise might as well join the Flat Earthers [a group of people who insist that the world is actually flat]. . . . My point of view is that many people do not want to know the truth about the Shroud and one finds oneself in front of an extraordinary spectacle of mass autosuggestion."[317] At least one member of STURP accepted the findings. Despite grave reservations about the revised protocol, Eric Jumper, who considered the carbon-dating to constitute the final word, expressed a belief that even if the original protocol had been followed, the results would have shown a medieval dating.[318]

Gonnella, who was widely blamed for ditching the original protocol, was defensive. "Scientifically I would have been happier and my mind at ease," he had said at the October press conference, "if the dating operation had been carried out in the context of comprehensive, wide-ranging, and thorough chemical and physical investigation of the Shroud as had been originally planned." So, why had he been a party to the change of protocol? At a conference the following May, Gonnella took a more strident, belligerent tone, charging that Michael Tite of the British Museum, who coordinated the project, as well as the representatives of the Oxford laboratory, lacking in professionalism and behaving like dogs, had insisted on changing the protocol, hoping, he said, that the Church officials would refuse these changes, "so that they could say that the Church was afraid of science." And so Tite, Hall, and others, "put us with our backs to the wall with their blackmail. Either we accepted the carbon 14 test with the conditions imposed by the laboratories or they would unleash

[a] campaign of accusations against the Church, saying [she] was afraid of truth and that [she] was an enemy of science."[319] Some made the charge that the decision to change the protocol came not so much from Tite and the laboratories but from Gonnella and Ballestrero.

The cardinal, taking a more moderate and conciliatory tone than his assistant, said, "I do not think . . . that the Church should question the results. . . . I do not think that . . . the Church should take the trouble of criticizing these most respectable scientists who up to now deserve only respect; nor would it be really proper to censor them because their results do not agree with the sentimental reasons that certain people may entertain."[320] Nevertheless, the following spring, when a journalist asked the pope whether he thought the Shroud was authentic, John Paul II answered, "I think it is."[321] Then next year, Vatican spokesman Joaquin Navarro Vals affirmed, "The result of the medieval dating has created a strange situation, one which contrasts with the preceding results that, however, were not contrary to a dating going back to two thousand years. This medieval dating is but one experimental result among others, which, having the validity and limits of separate tests, should be integrated into multidisciplinary tests."[322]

Vals indeed spoke for many, who believed that in light of the many earlier tests that seemed to indicate the Shroud's authenticity, something must have gone wrong with the carbon-dating. If the Shroud was medieval, how could it have been created? No one could suggest any *convincing* technique known in medieval — or even modern — times that could have made it possible for an image such as that seen on the Shroud to be faked. "We do not expect the captain of an Atlantic-crossing jumbo-jet, spotting that his fuel gauge suddenly read, 'Empty,' immediately to ditch his aircraft in the sea without a few further checks,"[323] was the comment of Ian Wilson.

Several years later, a survey was made in Italy of people visiting a photographic exhibit on the Shroud. Nearly thirteen hundred people were polled as to their opinion of the carbon-dating and the authenticity of the Shroud. The results: two percent said that the test was a failure and should be done over; three percent said the test should never have been done; five percent expressed their belief that the test was valid and should be accepted as final. Eleven percent conceded that they knew nothing of the Shroud. Fourteen percent were of the opinion that the Church should not have trusted the scientists, who were mainly non-Catholics. Twenty-six percent believed that the test was not done property. The largest group of those polled, thirty-nine percent, answered that they believed that "the test does not settle anything. Something must have gone wrong. Too many other proofs favor authenticity."[324]

The scientists who proposed the original protocols, while generally reluctant to criticize the integrity or competence of the scientists who did the testing, were, in fact, skeptical about the results of the carbon-dating. Of course, of greatest concern to them was the failure to follow the original protocols. They were also troubled that the dates of the control sample-cloths that were tested along with the Shroud were easily accessible to the laboratories. They were distressed also by the fact that the laboratories, or at least some individuals associated with them, had apparently violated the signed agreements and conferred with each other during the period of testing. Concern was greatest about the area where the sample was cut and the possibility of contamination.[325]

Textile expert Gilbert Raes complained that it was "unscientific" that "no experiments were done to determine the type and amount of cotton in the region of the samples." He deplored the lack of coordination among specialists. "I could have told them what to do," he insisted.[326]

Alan Adler, in an interview several years later, criticized the abandonment of the original protocol. He recalled that when it was drawn up, archaeologist William Meacham had "pointed out all the things you could screw up if you didn't have an archaeologist involved in the sampling, to advise you what to do and what not to do. And a chemist, to tell you what to do and what not to do before you start sampling. That was all in the original protocol. *They didn't follow it.* They wrote another protocol. *They didn't follow that.* When asked why they took the sample where they took it, the answer was: 'Well, it was cut there before.' Now that is the stupidest argument in the world for taking one sample from the place where they took it. Because they know that area is an area that's been repaired; they know it's in a water stain; they know it's by a scorch; and they know that people have found previous chemical evidence that area is peculiar. But nevertheless, that's what they did. And that's why we have a date that all sorts of people don't believe."[327] Adler felt that those who arranged the final protocol had acted carelessly, because "they were sure the date was going to come out right. . . . They were so sure that the date was going to come out right that they ignored all the things people told them about that . . . would screw it up."[328]

It is well-known that the radiocarbon-dating of an artifact can be affected by the substances that are on it or in it, but the scientists at the laboratories were confident that the Shroud sample had been sufficiently cleaned. Some of those who argued for the Shroud's authenticity wondered whether, if Jesus was in fact resurrected, this unique event would have affected the Shroud. Someone speculated that the resurrection might have bombarded the Shroud with a heavy dose of neutrons, and, when questioned at the International Scientific Symposium on the Shroud at Paris in September 1989, Michael Tite admitted that "the production of carbon 14 from the nitrogen present in the linen is certainly possible if someone has bombarded the Shroud with a strong dose of neutrons."[329] Most scientists, however, did not want to discuss this possibility, as it would involve a totally unique sort of contamination resulting from an event quite beyond the realm and scope of scientific investigation. Several scientists pointed, however, to some measurable factors that might have led to the contamination of the fabric.

Giovanni Riggi believed that the cloth could have been contaminated by the great quantities of smoke and dust to which it had been subjected over a period of many years. "It can be affirmed with certainty," he insisted, "as a result of the examination of numerous specimens [of dust taken from the Shroud] that the smoke from the heating systems over many centuries, and in particular, the last decades, could have insinuated itself into the weave, partly during the public and the private expositions (mostly held in the winter months) and partly during the times between the expositions by infiltrating through the openings in the reliquary. Another possible source for these dusts can be related to the illumination of the places when the expositions were held in olden times, for example, by the light of candles. . . . The reliquary that contains the cloth . . . is not airtight and allows the infiltration of contaminating particles, which is an all the more serious matter since the atmosphere pollution of the skies of Turin is greater."[330] Others pointed to the possibility of contamination from proteins and lipids from human sweat; mold, mildew, and other fungus growth; mites and other microscopic organisms; and hydrocarbon contaminations from decay productions from the cellulose of wooden frames.[331] Still others pointed to the fire at Chambery as a source of radiocarbon dating-altering contaminates. Paul Maloney, of the Association of Scientists and Scholars International for the Shroud of Turin, pointed out that the place from which the sample was taken had been, over the years, "handled very heavily. During ninety-nine percent of all exhibitions of the Shroud, clerics held it up for viewing using the two corners on the same side as the 'side strip' where the sample was taken."[332] Maloney also called attention to the fact that the corner from which the sample was taken "lay precisely in the area where the superheated water settled when the fire was doused to save the Shroud. Silver melts at nine hundred sixty degrees centigrade, so the Shroud must have been subjected to 'pressure-cooker conditions' which would have dissolved any contaminants and transported them into the very molecular structure of the flax fibers. . . . [Thus, the] carbon 14 contents of the Shroud would have been 'topped up' and [made to] appear younger than [indicated by the tests]."[333]

Michael Tite, at the 1989 symposium, insisted that his critics were simply grasping at straws. Contamination would have to amount to at least sixty percent of the material to affect the carbon-dating, and this, he felt, was virtually impossible.[334] Alan Adler was not so dogmatic. Asked if carbon from the surface contamination could have been forced into the chemical makeup of the cellulose fibers during the Chambery fire, he replied, "Not very likely. To have the date be over one thousand years off, you'd have to replace forty percent of the carbons by modern carbon, to get the right ratio (of C-12 to C-14) to make it turn out right." He conceded however, "Now if you have some crazy mechanism involving kinetic isotope effects that would selectively replace C-14 atoms, then it would take a much smaller percentage."[335] But what was this mechanism?

What made many students of the Shroud especially skeptical of the carbon 14 dating was the fact that every other test to which the fabric had been subjected — as well as its documented history — indicated an origin, if not in the first century, certainly long before the dates indicated by the three laboratories. Archaeologist Eugenia Nitowsk, who did not accept the carbon 14 dating as authoritative, observed, "In any form of inquiry or scientific discipline, it is the weight of evidence which must be considered conclusive. In archaeology, if there are ten lines of evidence, carbon-dating being one of them, and it conflicts with the other nine, there is little hesitation to throw out the carbon-date as inaccurate due to unforeseen contamination."[336] Ian Wilson argued, "In the case of the Shroud, the carbon 14 test proved little if anything. If we do not yet know how the image was formed, we cannot totally rule out the possibility of errors in the reading of the test due to a number of reasons. I am not questioning the competence of the laboratories that performed the test, nor that they genuinely arrived at a fourteenth century date, but like all carbon 14 tests serious experts, I feel strongly that the radiocarbon analysis should not be the only, and certainly not the final, arbiter to determine the date of origin of any given archaeological artifact."[337]

Accordingly, the Association of Scientists and Scholars International for the Shroud of Turin drew up a position paper. ASSIST was a group of scientists organized in 1983 that included archaeologists, botanists, chemists, computer experts, geologists, physicists, physicians, forensics experts, historians, experts in the study of coins, and archivists who, in their own words, wanted "to introduce the dimension of peer review into the field of sindonology." This is how they responded to the carbon testing:

"1. Given that the image on the Shroud of Turin has not been conclusively demonstrated to have been produced by an artist, that if painted it is not in the artistic style of [the Middle Ages] and

"2. Given that at least three researchers [Adler, Heller, and Baima Bollone] believe that chemical studies indicate the presence of blood in the Shroud, and

"3. Given that STURP has accumulated evidence that the Shroud contained the corpse of a crucified victim, and that crucifixion was not practiced since the fourth century, and

"4. Given that the Shroud contains medical information believed by many respected medically trained observers as medically accurate, which details do not reflect the medical knowledge available in the fourteenth century, and

"5. Given that there has, as yet, been no convincing demonstrable mechanism offered for the presence of the three-dimensional information coded on the Shroud, and

"6. Given the pollen information on the Shroud implies the presence of the cloth, at one point in its history, in Israel, a position currently supported by specialists in palynology and botany in Israel, and

"7. Given the historical evidence appears to support that a cloth fitting or similar to the description of the Shroud of Turin was extant at least as early as the seventh century, we therefore conclude that the new information relating to the date appears to be in serious conflict with the larger body of scientific and historical data collected since 1898. While we acknowledge that numerous facets of the above points deserve careful examination, we would like to make the following observations about the carbon-dating test just completed:

"1. No detailed and extensive chemistry has ever been conducted to determine the kinds of contaminants present on the Shroud, methods of such detection, and methods of their removal complete with scientific controls for the same.

"2. There was no peer review by the radiocarbon community of the three-lab plan prior to the radiocarbon tests.

"3. There was no random selection of sample sites [on the Shroud]; at least two other sites ought to have been carbon-dated, and such sample as was tested came from one of the most contaminated places on the Shroud and may represent an anomaly; sites beneath the patches [sewn on after the 1532 fire], effectively protected since April 17, 1534, were bypassed for testing.

"4. There was no blind testing; each test sample was delivered to each laboratory completely intact, and each control cloth identified as to the century within which its date should fall."

Therefore, because the carbon-date was in conflict with other research, the members of ASSIST called for further scientific investigation. "Either the Shroud of Turin must be explained in terms of the fourteenth century date (in which case scientific investigation should be able to discover conclusive evidence that it was a painting), or a new investigation should uncover the reasons for the carbon 14 results obtained." According, they proposed (1) extensive scientific testing concerning "the nature of the cloth," with attention given to factors that might have affected the carbon-dating and to procedures to identify contaminants and ensure their removal prior to further testing; (2) the exploration of other methods to date the cloth, such as an attempt to detect the presence of copper in the area of the image of the eyes, where previous research indicated the presence of coins; (3) a meeting of scientists to discuss all facets of carbon tests [of 1988] and evaluate the results; and finally, (4) new radiocarbon testing, this time "guaranteed by rigorous scientific controls," with samples taken from at least three areas of the Shroud.[338] "When one body of scientific data conflicts with another," the paper read, "it is the domain of science to address the issues and resolve them with proper testing and peer review. We encourage this process to become a public one, so that Shroud research can become a truly reviewed field of endeavor."[339]

During the next several years two theories were advanced to explain why the laboratories that carried out the carbon-dating arrived at a medieval date. In 1994, Dmitri Kouznetsov, a former winner of the Lenin Prize for Science, working along with Andrey Ivanov at the Sedov Biopolymer Research Laboratory of Moscow, announced that he could guarantee that the Shroud was at least six hundred fifty years older than the carbon-dating indicated that it was. This was because of two factors: the Chambery fire and the way flax was processed in ancient times.

Kouznetsov and Ivanov believed that the fire released gases containing carbon monoxide and carbon dioxide, which, along with the high temperature, caused what is known as an isotopic exchange. This, in turn, increased by twenty percent the amount of carbon 14 in the cloth. The action of the melting silver from the superheated reliquary would have enhanced this effect. The Russian researchers studied artifacts recovered from the ruins of Pompeii, and noted that materials that were burned in close proximity to silver objects seemed to have a slower process of decay.[340]

Kouznetsov experimented with samples of ancient linen, the age of which was well-established, and subjected them to conditions which he believed to be similar to those that prevailed in the 1532 fire. Then he had the samples carbon-dated. In every instance the reading indicated that the cloth was much younger than it actually was.[341] For example, he took a piece of linen cloth dating to first century Palestine, subjected it to conditions he thought likely in the fire, and got a carbon-dating of A.D. 1200.[342] This was apparently the sample in which there was the greatest discrepancy between the known date of the sample and the date given in the carbon-dating. Most of the objects he tested, under the conditions to which he subjected him, gave a date about six hundred fifty years too "young."

Although the conditions generated by the fire might skew the carbon-date of the Shroud by several *hundred* years, they would probably not alter the results by over a *thousand* years. In order to generate a date a thousand years off, most experts believed that there would have to be a forty percent increase in carbon 14. The Russians could account for only a twenty percent increase. Kouznetsov came up with another theory that would result in further date correction. It was the concept of "biofractionation." He felt that he had reason to believe that the process by which linen was manufactured from flax in ancient times triggered accumulations of bacteria that increased the carbon 14 content of the cloth.[343]

Three scientists from the laboratory in Arizona that had participated in the carbon-dating tried to reproduce the effect Kouznetsov and Ivanov described and failed to do so, denouncing the Russians' "attack" on the carbon-dating "unsubstantiated and incorrect."[344] On the other hand, Alan Adler told an interviewer that the forty percent carbon exchange that most scientists insisted was necessary to push the date of the Shroud back to the first century "need not be so." A smaller percentage could have the same effect if "another kind of kinetic isotope effect" occurred, not from the biology of living plants, but from chemical reactions during the fire. The problem is, however, nobody will ever know for sure the conditions of the Chambery fire.[345] John Jackson tends to be supportive of the work of the Russian researchers. His research, he said in an interview in 1997, "tend to confirm Kouznetsov-Ivanov." He found that their data can be explained by a mathematical model, but wanted "independent experiments," asserting, "We always reserve the right to change our mind."[346]

In September 1994, a "Round Table on the Microbiology of Ancient Artifacts" was held in San Antonio, Texas. Here Dr. Leoncio Garza-Valdes, a physician in the Department of Microbiology at the Texas Health Science Center at San Antonio, presented another theory. He called attention to the presence of "bioplastic coatings" produced by bacteria and fungi, which are found on the surface of ancient artifacts and around the fibers of ancient textiles. These bacteria, he argued, could add to the carbon 14 content of the object on which they were found. Garza-Valdes obtained from Giovanni Riggi a small sample of cloth from the Shroud, taken from the same area from which the carbon-dating was done. Looking at it under the microscope he found that there was in fact a bioplastic coating "of varying thickness" around the fibers. The cleaning method employed by the laboratories in 1988 had failed to remove this coating and Garza-Valdes and his associates were convinced that it was this bioplastic coating that had added carbon 14 to the cellulose of the Shroud and thrown off the carbon-dating. He was unable to specify the extent to which the carbon-dating was skewed.[347] He speculated that the cloth in the area where it was most handled might be contaminated by as much as sixty percent, which even the skeptical Edward Hall of Oxford admitted would be enough to skew the dating.[348]

Harry Gove, who helped develop the AMS method of carbon-dating and who was involved in the testing in 1988, believed (in 1996) that Garza-Valdes' research needed to be taken seriously.[349] In fact, Garza-Valdes invited him to study the Shroud thread, and when he did, Gove stated that he was "convinced of the general validity of Garza-Valdes's findings." There was in fact "some sort of 'halo' of bioplastic coatings around some of the threads."[350]

John Jackson was skeptical. In 1997 he expressed his doubts that there was enough bioplastic material on the Shroud "that would skew the carbon-dating by any significant factor." His own calculations did not support the Texan's theory.[351] Adler was also skeptical.[352]

Adler, in the meantime, had carried out tests to determine whether the "obviously contaminated sample" was truly representative of the rest of the cloth. Along with two colleagues the chemist carried out additional spectroscopic investigation of samples from the STURP sticky tapes. In a 1996 article he wrote, "Nineteen assorted fibers representative of non-image, waterstain, scorch, image, backing cloth, and serum coated fibers were extracted from the tapes and characterized by previously reported methods." These were then compared with fifteen single fibers taken from three threads from the radiocarbon sample. In addition, two blood samples were taken from the tapes and "compared against several types of blood controls." These blood controls included two *simulacra*: "a traumatic blood exudate (whole blood diluted with bilirubin-enriched human albumin) and mineral simulated blood (iron oxide, cinnabar, and a trace of calcite suspended in gelatin)." The samples were examined by a process known as "Fourier Transform Infrared Microspectrophotometry" and the fibers were scanned with an electron microprobe. In addition, ultraviolet visible spectrophotometry was also used to study dried films of the two blood *simulacra*. The typical Fourier Transform Infrared absorbance patterns of the single fibers samples were "all distinguishably different from each another, clearly indicating differences in their chemical composition." These differences were "further confirmed by peak frequency analysis utilizing the computer software that generates the spectral data." The researchers found that "in particular the radiocarbon samples are not representative of the non-image samples that comprise the bulk of the cloth." Moreover, scanning electron microprobe data showed "gross enrichment of the inorganic mineral elements in the radiocarbon samples, even compared to the water stain fibers taken from the bulk of the cloth." Adler wrote, "In fact, the radiocarbon fibers appear to be an exaggerated composite of the water stain and scorch fibers, thus confirming the physical location of the suspect radiosample site and demonstrating that it is not typical of the non-image sections of the main cloth." [353]

Drawing upon the researches of Alan Whanger of Duke, also pointed out that image analysis studies comparing the blood marks on the Shroud with those of the Cloth of Oviedo, (a cloth alleged to be the *sudarium*, or "handkerchief," which was placed on the head of the dead Jesus, which can be traced historically to the seventh century A.D.), also cast doubts on the accuracy of the carbon-dating. The blood images on the Cloth of Oviedo are similar to those on the Shroud. When compared, the dorsal head-wound marks of both cloths show complex patterns of wounds which are so similar as to "suggest that these two cloths were in contact with the same wounded body, presumably within the same short time period."[354]

And so, the radiocarbon-dating of the Shroud under a protocol challenged by nearly all scientists familiar with the cloth, did, in fact, lead (as one carbon-dating expert had predicted) to "enormous controversy [and] endless disputes and recriminations."

Chapter XI

The Forgery Theories

Some have no difficulty accepting either the results of the 1988 carbon-dating or the idea that the image was created by an artist or craftsman during the Middle Ages. Even before the carbon-testing, some scholars doubted that the Shroud of Turin had once enfolded the body of Jesus. As we have seen, there were several reasons for this. First of all, the Scriptures do not give a detailed description of the burial clothing in which Jesus was wrapped. The Greek used by St. John *can* be translated in such a way as to suggest that Jesus was laid out, not in a cloth of one piece, like the Shroud, but in strips, like an Egyptian mummy (although the fourth Gospel *can* also be translated in a way to make the description of the grave clothes consistent with the appearance of the Shroud). Second, there is some question about the provenance of the Shroud. Although there are several clear references to a cloth, preserved first at Edessa, then at Constantinople, which generally fits the description of the Shroud, there is no *proof* that the Mandylion and the Shroud were one and the same object. Moreover, refer-

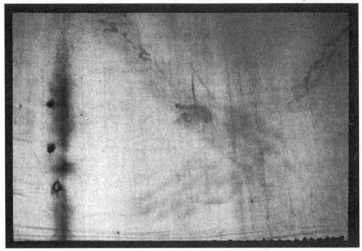

Photos from 1973 showing the wrist wound (above) and the arms and the wound in the side (below).

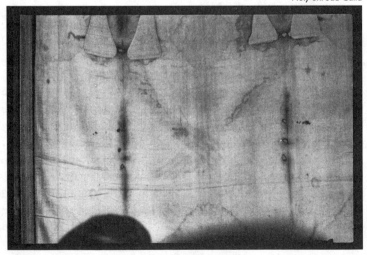

ences to the Mandylion before the sixth century are extremely scanty and uncertain (but so are references to just about anything from the late Roman Empire and early Middle Ages). Third, although the custody of the Shroud of Turin can be traced, without question, to the de Charny family in fourteenth-century France, there exists, from the same period, the correspondence of Bishop Pierre d'Arcis, who insisted that the Shroud was a fake. (However, just because one individual is convinced that a particular object is a fake does not necessarily mean that it is.)

In addition, some buttress their skepticism by pointing out that the man depicted on the Shroud does not look natural to them. Joe Nickell objected that the man, who was about six feet tall, was unrealistically large. As we have seen, if the few skeletal remains recovered intact from an ancient cemetery in Israel are representative, the man of the Shroud would have been tall for his time and place, but not unusually so. Besides, if one is inclined to see the man of the Shroud as a medieval forgery, there still remains the problem that medieval Europeans were, on the average, not as tall as modern people, either.

Skeptics have noted that one arm appears longer than the other; the head appears disembodied; the face looks unnaturally long and thin. All of these features have been explained by those who believe that the image is authentic as the result of either the position of the body or the lay of the cloth. Some found it significant that the man's hands are discreetly crossed over his loins, so that the private parts are not in evidence. One writer, noting this, observed, "Looks suspiciously like a concession to medieval prudery."[355] Lynn Pincknett and Clive Prince observed that the position of the hands "seems an unusual way to lay out a corpse" and seemed to them to indicate that "the cloth was intended for display in order to avoid offending the sensibilities of the faithful." They furthermore proposed that the genitals were missing in an effort to avoid depicting, in the name of accuracy, a circumcised Jesus. This, they argued, would have offended medieval Christians, who were uncomfortable with a "reminder of the Jewishness of their Lord."[356] Another author even suggested that the serene expression on the face was strange for a person tortured to death.

James Druzik, an art conservator associated with the Getty Conservation Institute in Marina del Ray, California, offered his theory that the image must have occurred by accident. Pointing out that he knew of many artifacts that have "transfer stains on their surfaces that were unintentional," he explained that some stains occur "from decomposition . . . from wood to paper to textile." This he said, is "so common it's not even remarkable." He theorized that the image on the Shroud *might* have been caused by "a carved wooden icon." In the Middle Ages, Druzik declared, people had "virtually no education by our standards. . . . You were spooked by anything you didn't understand. If you had a piece of linen draped over a wooden icon, and you came back ten years later and found an image appearing on it, you'd be totally freaked out."[357] There are two significant problems with this theory. First, no one has identified the mechanism for this "transfer." Second, no one can explain the anatomical accuracy of the image, which, if a work of art, would make it unique in history.

Almost no artists or scientists agreed with McCrone in his insistence on a painted Shroud. For instance, Leo Vala, a photographer specializing in 3-D and movie photography, declared around 1991 that "No one could have faked that image. No one could do it today with all the technology we have. It's a perfect negative. It has a photographic quality that is extremely precise."[358] In 1990, Carlo Carra, a respected Italian artist, insisted, "If a painter were ever to try to portray the face of the dead Christ with all the marks left on it by the savage treatment inflicted on Him before and during the crucifixion, he would only end up with a monstrous-looking portrait. . . . Astoundingly, the entire battered body of this crucified man is portrayed on the Shroud with a realism whose precision is uncanny. But what is positively incredible is that a would-be artist could create this image as a negative. No artist could as much as conceive such a task. I do not know what mystery lies behind the Shroud, but this much I know: no artist's brush has touched the Shroud."[359]

Peter Rinaldi recounted that two artists from Turin made replicas of the Shroud, working directly from the original. When they were photographed, the positive versions were a "disappointment" and the images on the negative were "so distorted as to be barely recognizable."[360]

Jackson pointed out that the anatomical exactness of the bloodstains virtually ruled out the possibility that the image been painted or sculpted in the Middle Ages, or, for that matter, at any other time. He pointed out the correlation of the blood trickle off the foot in the dorsal image with a blood mark of similar size and shape next to the foot region in the frontal image. "In our experiments where a volunteer subject was enfolded in a full-scale model of the Shroud with an image upon it," he wrote in 1991, "we found . . . that [the two blood marks] align directly over another. This cannot be a coincidence nor the result of a super-sophisticated artist who anticipated such detail. This congruence strongly suggests that the Shroud was folded lengthwise over the head of a body and that the feet were wrapped so as to bring the dorsal bloodstream into contact with the frontal end of the cloth where the blood residue was transferred."

The physicist also pointed out many bloodstains "which correspond to distinctly different flow directions, consistent with a vertical crucifixion first, followed by a horizontal burial of a real corpse." He found that the vertical bloodstains corresponded to clot transfers and to earlier flows that had partially dried. The horizontal flows, however, "depict liquid, and therefore, presumably late time post-mortem flows."

Jackson also noted that the bloodstain on the wrist "provides an independent confirmation that the flow-path was in the direction of gravity." Ultraviolet fluorescence photography of the clot on the wrist revealed "a clear halo emanating into the cloth." This, he asserted, could be explained as a natural separation of serum from the blood during clotting. Then, if the two streams of blood on this wrist were positioned "as to be in the downward direction of gravity, the accompanying hand and forearm assume a crucifixion position."

All these things Jackson characterized as "subliminal details," observable only through scientific tests not available in the Middle Ages. Another such detail was microscopic dust found on the dorsal foot imprint, and only there — an indication that the man portrayed on the cross had walked barefoot shortly before his execution. It was scarcely conceivable that these features could have been the work of an artist, because they would have been impossible for even the artist to see them and there was no reason to include them since no one else could see them, either.[361]

Some Shroud skeptics believed that the image was produced by means of scorching the cloth with a heated statue. Robert Wild, a Jesuit scholar, believed even before the cloth was carbon-dated that an artist scorched a linen cloth "with a properly heated statue, or more likely, a pair of bas-reliefs, using whole blood to create appropriate stains." He felt that the inability of modern experimenters to achieve this effect without damaging the cloth was simply due to the fact that the technique, obviously known in the Middle Ages, has since been lost.[362] Edward Hall, who was part of the team that carbon-dated the Shroud in Oxford, was convinced that the image was the "result of a scorch done cleverly with a poker or as a bas relief using a heated statue."[363] Since the 1970s, the foremost advocate of the scorch theory has been Joe Nickell, who as we have already seen insisted that a forger created the image on the Shroud by placing a wet sheet over a bas-relief covered with iron oxide and then adding bloodstains. Nickell also insisted that it would have taken only about two days to shape the image out of clay and two more to produce the image and add the flagellation marks and bloodstains. "The artist could work out any problems directly on the relief, making as many corrections as desired with trial prints on cheap cloth at each stage, until satisfactory results were obtained."[364] Although he was, in fact, able to produce body images using his proposed technique, there were major differences between his productions and the image on the Shroud. For one thing, the discoloration on the Shroud penetrates less than three fibers, while the coloring Nickell applied to his experimental cloths soaked the entire fabric. Again, a scorch will glow under ultraviolet light, and while the scorches on the Shroud from the 1532 do indeed fluoresce, the body image does not.[365] Researchers who studied Nickell's technique and work concluded that he was unable to produce "a superficial, highly resolved image with the Shroud's density shading and uniform intensity."[366]

Randall Bresee and Emily Craig of the University of Tennessee in an article in *Journal of Imaging Science and Technology* in 1994 described how they made a life-sized Shroud copy through a "burnishing technique." Ian Wilson, in *The Blood and the Shroud*, described how they painted it onto a piece of paper or vellum using "finely powdered iron-oxide-in-collagen binding medium," then placed the painted paper image face downward onto an identically sized piece of linen, rubbing vigorously with a wooden spoon from the non-image side, thus burnishing the mirror image onto the linen as they would a brass rubbing. Wilson described their efforts as a "superficial resemblance to the Shroud" without the Shroud's photographic quality and three-dimensionality.[367] Mark Borkan, a student of mathematics, in an article on the Shroud in *Vertices: The Duke University Magazine of Science, Technology, and Medicine*, commented that Craig and Bresee's methods were "grossly incapable of rendering an image with anywhere near the resolution of that on the Shroud." In fact, the Tennessee researchers admitted in their paper that it was "impossible to satisfy simultaneously all observations reported for the Turin image."[368]

Artist Isabel Piczek, a draftsman and muralist with the Construction Art Center of Los Angeles, argued that any image made by any sort of "impression methods" with a statue or relief always produce "great horizontal expansion [of the image] and distortion, which is radically absent from the Shroud's lean long figure." Moreover, she insisted, "Nobody in the Middle Ages could have made a statue that life-like and anatomically correct" and that "the heating methods and their controls in the Middle Ages were very poor" and incapable of the delicate precision necessary for producing such an image.[369]

Borkan described what a forger would have had to do to create the image on the Shroud. He would have had "medical and archaeological knowledge several centuries ahead of his . . . time." He would have incorporated into his image "the peculiarities of hundreds of Byzantine icons and other artistic productions scattered about an area larger than the Roman Empire" and also demonstrated knowledge of Jewish burial practices. He would have had to obtain a cloth that contained deposits of pollen from Palestine, from the environs of Edessa, from Constantinople, as well as from southern Europe. Moreover, he would have had to transfer cloth with actual blood and serum and place them accurately on the cloth without any image to work with. "The image the artist produced would have a perfect negative encoded with information about a body enfolded in it that . . . could not even be seen at close range."[370]

Some skeptics, forced to rule out the possibility that the image was a painting or the impression of a heated statue, have argued that a criminal artist actually crucified a Jewish man to create the model for his image. Others have suggested that during the crusades Moslems crucified a crusader as an intended insult to his religion. First of all, since crucifixion was not practiced in medieval times, the forger-criminal would have had to experiment in crucifying people in order to perfect his technique. Experiments even on the cadavers of those who had died naturally were forbidden in Christendom at the time, and it is highly unlikely that the forger could have carried on his work by torturing and killing dozens of people without attracting notice. Even if he escaped detection, he would have had to select victims with facial features that incorporated the features found on Byzantine icons. Moreover, he would still have to acquire a pollinated burial shroud and buried his victim according to first-century Jewish practices. He would have had to place soil on his victim's heel that contained substances peculiar to the caves of Palestine. This still could not account for the formation of the image. "It does not take a coroner to know that dead bodies don't produce images on cloth,"[371] Borkan wrote. The murderous artist would have to be quick at his work. The body on the Shroud shows no signs of decay, which would have been hastened, pathologists say, by open wounds. After thirty hours, "the emission of ammoniacal gases from the oral cavity" would have made a stain around the imprint of the lips, which is not there on the Shroud.[372] In addition, no one has ever figured out how the body was removed from the sheet without altering the stains.[373] The forger-criminal would have to have arrived at a technique, unknown even in the late twentieth century, of removing the body from the sheets without altering the image. No one has figured out how this could have been done. Even if the mechanism that made the image were accounted for, most scientists question whether the body — if such it was — could have been unwrapped without causing some damage or alteration to the image.

Other theories have been advanced by those who hold that the Shroud is a medieval creation. Noemi Gabrielli, former director of the art galleries of Piedmont, Italy, who was a member of the commission that examined the Shroud in 1973 and insisted at the time that it was the work of an artist who used techniques of shading associated with Leonardo da Vinci, later argued that the Shroud was in fact probably created by Leonardo da Vinci himself. The artist and inventor was not born until 1452 — a century after the cloth can be established, without a doubt, as the property of the de Charny family of Lirey — but Gabrielli found a "similarity in the technique and spirituality" between the face on the Shroud and the face of Christ in the Last Supper, and contended that the House of Savoy must have substituted the old Shroud with one made by Leonardo.[374]

This argument was further developed by Lynn Pincknett, editor of the *Macmillan Encyclopedia of the Paranormal,* who with co-author Clive Prince wrote *Turin Shroud: In Whose Image? The Truth Behind the Centuries-Long Conspiracy of Silence*, published in 1994 by HarperCollins. Among other things, they challenged the three-dimensional qualities of the VP-8 image of Jackson and Jumper, claiming that the two scientists "may have been prejudiced by their Catholic faith and membership of the Holy Shroud Guild," and arguing, "It would seem that the measurements of the man on the Shroud were adjusted to create the VP-8 image, especially in order to make the shorter face fit the back of the head, and to make the whole image an acceptable height."[375] They held that since carbon-dating has *proved* that the Shroud is not the burial sheet of Jesus and since other tests have shown that it is neither a painting nor the imprint of a statue, it must have been a sort of primitive photograph made by Leonardo da Vinci. They claimed that the celebrated artist was a likely member of a group called the Priory of Sion (which, they admit, has no records earlier than the nineteenth century). They furthermore speculated that, after Michelangelo turned down the job, the Pope commissioned Leonardo to create a better shroud.[376] This he did by crucifying a man, cutting off the head, and making a cast of the body. Then using a cast of his own head (which would account for the apparent absence of a neck in the Shroud image) he made a photograph using a wooden box known as a *camera obscura* with lenses or mirrors he prepared and a sheet he had treated with light-sensitive chemicals.[377] The authors moreover claimed that Leonardo surely subscribed to the beliefs of the Priory of Sion that Jesus did not die on the cross; that He was married to Mary Magdalene, who was in reality a high priestess of the Egyptian goddess Isis and the original Black Madonna. According to Pincknett and Prince, "the great Gothic cathedrals were dedicated to [Mary Magdalene]" rather than "the sexless goddess of the Virgin Mary."[378] In addition, they insisted that Jesus and the Magdalene had children who were part of a "magical" line. [379] The image, which is that of Leonardo, celebrates not Christ but John the Baptist, who was the founder of a religion of love associated with Isis.[380] The fact that Leonardo used his own face and someone else's body was a "visual pun saying to us across the centuries that the one who was beheaded [that is, John the Baptist] is 'over' one who was crucified. The blood is incongruously flowing from the wounds as if the man were still alive: here [Leonardo] is saying that Jesus never died on the cross, that he did not redeem anyone."[381] Pincknett and Prince maintain, "The image on the cloth is nothing less than a Iohnist hymn, celebrating the divine priesthood of John the Baptist in the cause of the real founder of the religion of love, the goddess Isis. In doing so, it also challenges the Church's age-old emphasis on male power, the superiority of priests and the submissiveness of women."[382]

The idea that Leonardo da Vinci would have been capable of producing the image on the Shroud was ridiculed by artist Isabel Piczek. Although he conceived of many devices that were not actually created for centuries, most of his inventions did not work. Piczek pointed out that Leonardo "designed an earth-digging machine. It would have taken two thousand men two and a half years to excavate as much as what two hundred men could have done in six months." Moreover, "He designed one cannon and weapon after the other, with principles which mankind reinvented centuries later, but they were all too big, required too many people to operate . . . and they were made from primitive materials, mostly wood. None of them went into production. He invented the bicycle, but made from wood. It did not work." Piczek went on to say that Leonardo, without understanding the laws of aerodynamics, "designed a flying machine resembling bat's wings." The flying machine did not work, either. He designed a method for the casting in a single piece of bronze of a huge equestrian statue of the Duke of Milan. "It was an ingenious plan, but one which did not work. His greatest masterpiece, *The Last Supper*, started to disintegrate within his own lifetime due to technical errors." Because Leonardo was usually unable to carry out his spectacular designs, Piczek argued that it seemed extremely unlikely that he could have created the Shroud.[383] None of Leonardo's notebooks, in which he evidently wrote down everything he thought or conceived or invented, ever mention a word about the Shroud of Turin. Despite the fact that Pincknett and Prince claim that there are Leonardo notebooks which have been lost, the fact remains that there is not a shred of historical documentation to support the theory that Leonardo created the Shroud any more than there is to back their novel historical and theological ideas. There is as much evidence to prove that Leonardo created the Shroud as there is that he built the pyramids.

The idea that the Shroud is a primitive photograph was further explored by Nicholas Allen, dean of the Faculty of Art and Design at Port Elizabeth Technikon, in Port Elizabeth, South Africa. Allen proposed that the Shroud could have been created in the fourteenth century by an artist who used: (1) rock crystal; (2) silver salts; and (3) salt of ammonia (found in urine), all of which would have been available at the time. In his article entitled "Verification of the Nature and Causes of the Photo-negative Images on the Shroud of Lirey-Chambery-Turin" he argued that the Shroud "could have been" produced by a form of primitive photography. This "hypothetical photographic technique," Allen insisted ". . . is the only plausible explanation for the image formation on the Shroud . . . and indicates that people in the late thirteenth and fourteenth century were indeed privy to a photographic technology which was previously thought to be unknown."[384]

The South-African scholar constructed a device known as a *camera obscura*. The size of a typical living room, it was built so that no light could get in except through a small opening for a rock crystal lens. He closed this opening and prepared a cloth made to the same dimensions of the Shroud, and, folding it once across its width and soaking it in light-sensitive silver nitrate, hung it up inside the *camera obscura* fifteen feet from the lens. When the cloth dried it became a sort of unexposed film. Next he made a plastic cast of a living man of roughly the same size and shape of the man of the Shroud. Allen then suspended the statue in the sunlight fifteen feet in front of the lens. His object was to project the image of the statue through the lens onto the cloth. After several days the reflection of the statue imprinted a negative onto the cloth. Allen then closed his improvised shutter and turned the statue around so that the back faced the lens, which he opened for several more days in order to create a front and back image similar to that of the Shroud. So that the negative would not fade from exposure to light, Allen washed it in a solution of ammonia salts.[385]

Although the process devised by Professor Allen produced an image with many characteristics of that of the Shroud of Turin, some have questioned whether it really could have been carried out in the Middle Ages. Wilson questioned whether medieval artists could have created a body cast of the quality devised by Allen, and why, if they could, someone would have gone to the trouble and expense to produce a negative image that could not be fully appreciated — even to its creator — for another five centuries[386] and at a time when "a large proportion of the populace would have been very easily duped by a feather of the Archangel Gabriel or a phial of the last breath of St. Joseph?"[387]

Isabel Piczek rejected Allen's hypothesis. First of all, she argued, the *camera obscura* that figured prominently in both the theories of Allen and of Pincknett and Prince was not a primitive photo camera, but a device used by artists to aid in representing buildings and open space in perspective. Although it was used by the Greeks and the Romans, it was not used in the Middle Ages. While Allen argued that all the materials needed for making a photograph were available by the thirteenth century, Piczek pointed out that at the time the chemical properties of silver nitrate were unknown, and there was no knowledge of optics "or the properties of light employing a bi-convex, finely ground quartz lens." The medieval photographer would have had to know the properties of ultraviolet radiation "before electromagnetism was known at all" and he would have had to known how to stabilize his image through the use of ammonia. Since it was unlikely that medieval technicians could produce a body cast of the quality Allen devised, a real corpse would have been required, and would have to hang in the sun for fourteen days. Piczek pointed out that the image on the Shroud is of a corpse in a state of *rigor mortis* and the fact is that "corpses do not maintain rigor mortis [and] cannot hang fourteen days in the sun, or else you would not care to see what the camera obscura would bring in onto your canvas."[388]

Christopher Knight, a consumer psychologist, and Robert Lomas, an electric engineer and physicist, wrote a book published by Century Books in London in 1997, called *The Second Messiah: Templars, The Turin Shroud, and the Great Secret of Freemasonry.* The authors, both Freemasons, argued that in the time of Christ the priests of the Temple of Jerusalem, who were each called by the name of an angel such as Michael or Gabriel, ran a school for boys and a school for girls. To preserve in their purity the lines of Levi and David, "when each of the chosen girls had passed through puberty, one of the priests would impregnate her with the seed of the holy bloodline and, once pregnant, she would be married off to a respectable man to bring up the child." Mary, after bearing the child of a priest styled "Gabriel," was married off to the aged Joseph.[389] According to Knight and Lomas, before the destruction of Jerusalem by the Romans in A.D. 70 some of the priests escaped Jerusalem and settled in different countries, adopting the local religious practices, but still maintaining the bloodlines of "the messiah of David and the messiah of Aaron, who would one day establish the kingdom of God on earth, and, accordingly, begot a line of noble European families, descended from David and Aaron."[390] Jesus, according to this argument, was not divine, but a royal leader, and the idea of resurrection came from the apostle Paul's misunderstanding of the initiation ritual in which candidates for the dignity of "Soldiers of the Temple" were wrapped in a white burial shroud and subjected to a symbolic death, from which they were "raised" by means of a "sacred ritual."[391]

According to Knight and Lomas, the medieval crusading order, the Knights Templar, was associated with this secret priesthood. The image on the Shroud is not that of Jesus, but of Jacques de Molay, Grand Master of the Knights Templar, who was subjected to torture seven years before his execution at the hands of the French king after condemnation by the pope. According to the authors, Molay was nailed to the wall and scourged, then "placed on the same soft bed from which he had been dragged earlier that morning. His head and shoulders were supported to assist his laboured breathing and the injured man's morbid fluids — sweat and blood with high lactic acid content — ran freely over his entire body. . . . The sheet made full contact with the back of Molay's supine body so that the blood and sweat left a crude image on the cloth beneath him. The cloth on the front of the body draped over the high points and the evaporating sweat passed upwards to the Shroud. Being in a soft bed with pillows ensured that his head was raised and his waist and knees were bent, bringing his hands down to the top of his thigh."[392]

Knight and Lomas conclude that "all evidence strongly suggests that Jacques de Molay was widely considered by many to be a holy martyr, and by some to be the Second Messiah, who had, once again, been murdered by the Roman establishment." Many believed that the devastation that swept all of Christendom in the fourteenth century in the form of the Black Death and other disasters was the wrath of God. The Church, Knight and Lomas said, feared that the miraculous image of Molay that had appeared on the Shroud "would let out the terrible secret that they had crucified him too. They had to keep the identity of the Shroud image hidden or they would be swept away by a new cult of Molay, just like the cult of Jesus that created them in the first place. The problem was finally headed off by the Church accepting the public display of the Shroud and encouraging people to believe that it was the image of Christ, even though they had [at the time of the d'Arcis-de Charny affair] previously denied it."[393]

Of course, Knight and Lomas had not a shred of documentation for their contentions except Masonic traditions. Their claims do not square with the findings of nearly all medical experts that the man in the Shroud is *dead*. And they do not address the fact that at the time of his torture (of which we know few details), in contrast to the figure on the Shroud, who was clearly a man of no more than early middle age, Molay was sixty-three years old.

If none of the attempts to explain the Shroud image as an artistic creation of the Middle Ages or Renaissance seem satisfactory, we should turn to the explanations of those who argue that the image does in fact date to the time of Christ.

The Palace and Cathedral at Turin, Italy (below); the crowds gathering to view the shroud during the 1978 exposition (left).

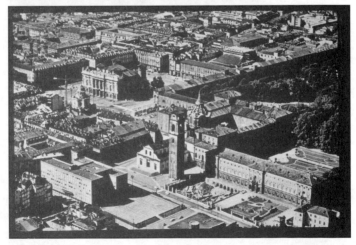

Chapter XII

The Continuing Mystery

The earliest theory offered to explain the formation of the image on the Shroud was put forward by French chemist and biologist Paul Vignon in 1902. He hypothesized that the image may have been produced by vapors from the body that was wrapped in the Shroud. Under great stress, he pointed out, people often produce sweat that contains a substance known as urea. This, he felt, is what happened to the man of the Shroud, whose body was drenched in a sweat that left a deposit rich in urea on his skin. When this came in contact with the sheet, which had been soaked in aloes (a spice mentioned in New Testament accounts of the burial of Christ), the urea fermented and produced ammonia, the vapors from which alkalized the aloes and discolored the cloth.[394]

Vignon's theory has been challenged by more recent researchers. The process the Frenchman described can indeed produce density shading similar to that seen on the Shroud, but the image resulting from it would not be nearly so clear and sharp. The cloth had to have been damp, and a damp cloth would cling to the body and produce an image that would permeate the entire cloth (as we have seen that the image on the Shroud does not). The vapor theory also makes it difficult to account for the "non-body images," such as those of the coins on the eyelids.[395]

Several scientists who supported the authenticity of the Shroud believed, like the skeptical Nickell, that the image was produced by some sort of contact. Giovanni Judica Cordiglia covered the face of a cadaver with a powdery mixture of equal parts aloe and myrrh, then applied a cloth soaked in a mixture of turpentine and olive oil in a proportion of two to one. Then he placed the cloth in a damp environment and produced "shaded images." Likewise, Ruggero Romanese permeated sheets with a mixture of powdered aloe and myrrh in equal parts and applied them to the faces of cadavers, some of which he dampened with water, others with "a physiological solution dispersed with a nebulizer." After a few minutes the aloe oxidized and an imprint began to form on the cloth. A third Italian researcher, Sebastiano Rodante, sprayed a solution made of eight to ten parts of sweat to one of blood onto a ceramic cast and then added equal parts of powdered aloe and myrrh. He then laid a linen cloth on the cast for thirty-six hours. He was able to obtain an image on the cloth in this way, and, in later experiments, obtained better results by soaking his cloths in a water solution of aloe and myrrh. The American Samuel Pellicori, a member of STURP, obtained an image on a cloth that he treated with very thin layers of sweat, olive oil, myrrh, or aloe, and then heated in an oven. The cloth yellowed and became dehydrated and oxidized, as in the image on the Shroud.[396] While all these procedures produced images, these images, like those made by Nickell, lacked the clarity of the Shroud image. "There is nothing in these images of the precision and detail we admire on the Shroud's imprints," Peter Rinaldi wrote. "The faces in these experiments are particularly disappointing, not to say, repulsive."[397]

John D. German, who performed experiments similar to those of Pellicori and the Italian researchers, pointed out difficulties with the contact theory: (1) the "sensitizing substance" would saturate the entire image, and there are no areas on saturation on the image on the Shroud; (2) in the areas where the first contact took place, "the intensities," were all the same, but on the Shroud they are not; and (3) in the experiments the dorsal image was affected by the weight of the body, but in the image on the Shroud it apparently was not."[398]

Optical crystallographer Joseph Kohlbeck and archaeologist Eugenia Nitowski had another theory, based on their examination of limestone samples from Jerusalem. With distilled water they made a paste of the Jerusalem limestone, which was mildly alkaline because of the presence of small amounts of calcium oxide or hydroxide. Then they lightly rubbed this paste into new linen fibers. They found that the slightly alkaline aragonite attacked the outer skin of the fibers and produced a yellowish color very similar to the color of the fibers of the Shroud. Kohlbeck and Nitowski proposed, "The small amounts of iron in the Jerusalem limestone carried with the water are responsible for the yellowish color. The process by which this slightly alkaline limestone attacks the outer skin of the fibers is known as mercerization." They theorized that "the extreme body heat produced by crucifixion may have resulted in a mercerization process that produced the image by interaction with the mildly alkaline aragonite containing traces of iron." This process would account for the fact that the frontal image is clearer and contains more detail than the dorsal image: "If the shrouded, crucified body was placed on a limestone tomb bench for further preparation, the back of the body would have been in contact with the cold, wet limestone, resulting in cooling and increased moisture. Cooling would have slowed or stopped the image-forming process. The front of the body, on the other hand, would have remained warm longer, allowing the formation of the image through the mercerization on the moist, slightly alkaline cloth." In the 1980s Kohlbeck and Nitowski reported, "We have begun to perform some experimental work to test these theories, but the results are by no means conclusive and much work remains to be done."[399]

A man by the name of Natale Noguier de Malijay in 1930 was first to speculate that that image on the Shroud was formed as the result of a "photoflash" connected with the resurrection of Christ.[400] Along these same lines, an English writer named Geoffrey Ashe, some three decades later, suggested, "The physical change of the body at the resurrection may have released a brief and violent burst of some radiation other than heat — perhaps scientifically identifiable, perhaps not — which scorched the cloth."[401] In 1978, Ray Rogers of STURP was quoted in the *Los Alamos Monitor:* "I am forced to conclude that the image was formed by a burst of radiant energy — light, if you will."[402] Researchers, however, have used flash and laser, heat, and radiation in futile attempts to reproduce the characteristics of the Shroud on test cloths.[403]

Thomas J. Phillips, formerly of Harvard University's High Energy Physics Laboratory, was associated with Fernilab in Batavia, Illinois, in 1988 when, in the same issue of *Nature* that published the results of the carbon-dating, he suggested that the Shroud might have been bombarded by neutrons at the resurrection of Christ. The image looks like a scorch and he speculated that the resurrecting body might have radiated neutrons which irradiated the Shroud and changed "some of the nuclei to different isotopes by neutron capture."[404] Some of the neutrons would have been captured by carbon 13 to become carbon 14, and thus raise the amount of carbon 14 in the cloth, "making it appear to be younger than it actually is."[405] Phillips conceded, "If the Shroud is in fact the burial cloth of Christ . . . then according to the Bible it was present at a unique physical event: the resurrection of a dead body." Phillips conceded, however, "Unfortunately, this event is not accessible to scientific scrutiny."[406] Adler said of Phillips, "He's a theoretician. . . . And he actually suggested a way [the theory] can be tested. He pointed out that if that's what happened, you look at a ratio of chlorine isotopes. That fact is, nobody has looked. It's an experiment that calls for fairly large pieces of sample. So here's a theoretical explanation that would work, but it hasn't been tested."[407] The Phillips theory is not accepted by most scientists. "Unless you can reproduce the Resurrection," said John Heller, "the entire neutron theory goes down the tubes."[408]

A chemist named Giles Carter explained that "moderately strong x-rays" that emanated from the bones of the man of the Shroud would have been absorbed by "elements [such as sodium, silicon, phosphorus, potassium, and calcium] at the surface of the body." These would then fluoresce and admit secondary x-ray images of long wave length. His theory accounts for the "sudden shifts of intensity" seen on the image, which most attribute to differences in the lots of thread that were used to manufacture the cloth, but which he attributes to variations in the concentration of iron in the Shroud.[409] This would also account for the long fingers and wide eyes of the man on the Shroud, which are, in part, actually images of the finger-bones and eye-orbits.

Thaddeus Trenn, of the University of Toronto, developed a theory of "Weak Dematerialization," based on Carter's research. He argued that the "pion bonding holding the nucleons together" would have been overcome by energy input into the body, leading to "dematerialization associated with spontaneous pion decay," which, in turn, would cause the emission of x-rays from the deep structure of the body and "coronal discharge [the emission of ionized particles in a high-energy field] by free electrons." The x-radiation and coronal discharge, Trenn declared, could account for "both a superficial and highly resolved image." Again, the cause for the dematerialization cannot be explained in scientific terms. Alan Adler called the Carter theory and, by implication, that of Trenn, "Great physically, great chemically, but absolute bizarre biologically."[410]

None of the many theories that have been advanced to explain the image on the Shroud have found wide acceptance. Orazio Petrosillo and Emanuela Marinelli pointed out that nearly every mechanism for the formation of the image that has been proposed has managed to explain some, but not all, of the characteristics of the imprint. "The problem," they argued, "is that the explanations that could be upheld from a chemical point of view are excluded by physics, and, on the contrary, some physical explanations that might be plausible are completely excluded by chemistry." When the image was formed, "all the hypothesized phenomena" described in the vapor, contact, and photoflash theories "contributed in some part, though in a manner not yet known."[411] Physicist John Jackson, in fact, said, "On the basis of physico-chemical processes known hitherto, we would have good reason to say that the image of the Shroud cannot exist, but it is real even though we cannot explain how it was formed."[412]

Jackson himself advanced his own tentative hypothesis in a paper he presented at a conference in St. Louis in 1991. He noted that chemical tests of the yellow fibrils showed that the color was due to "a dehydration phenomenon," similar to the process in which linen is discolored when scorched by a hot iron. "That is not to say that the body image was, in fact, set onto the cloth by heat," he said, "but only that the chemistry of the fibrils composing the Shroud image appears to be similar to that caused by scorching." Scorching, however, typically causes the discoloration of the entire thickness of the cloth, as in the case of the burns from the 1532 fire. The body image, however, does not penetrate the cloth, but is "entirely superficial."[413]

Likewise he noted that the finger-bones of the man of the Shroud were visible "well into the palm of the hands" and that "the thickness of the fingers" was "individually preserved well into the palm of the hand." Thus, "it . . . seems as though we are looking at the internal skeletal structure of the hand imaged through the intervening flesh tissues onto the Shroud cloth."[414] Searching for a way to explain this, he suggested, "Perhaps the time has come to ask if we ought to start thinking about the Shroud image in categories quite different from those that have been considered in the past. . . . Perhaps we need to be more flexible in our scientific approach and consider hypotheses that might not be found readily in conventional modern science; for it is conceivable that the Shroud image represents . . . some type of 'new physics' that ultimately requires an extensions or even revision of current concepts."[415]

The physicist then made the following inferences:

1. The body and blood images were formed directly from a human body that was enveloped in the Shroud.

2. Gravity was a significant factor in the production of the image. "Whatever mechanism was involved in producing the Shroud image," he asserted, "must have had the property of transferring body surface information in the vertical-only position."

3. The Shroud was in two different draping configurations

when the body images were formed. The initial configuration "corresponds to the way in which a cloth would drape naturally over a human face," but when the body image was produced, "the Shroud apparently deformed for some reason to a somewhat flatter draping configuration, the result of which laterally positioned the images of the sides of the face several centimeters inside the bloodstain pattern."[416]

Therefore, he reasoned, the Shroud at first covered a body shape, but that the body, for some reason, "did not impede the collapse of the Shroud during the time of image formation . . . *into and through* the underlying body structure."[417] The body seemed to have become "transparent" to its physical surroundings and "a stimulus was generated that recorded the passage of the cloth through the body region onto the cloth as an image." It was "unclear in an *a priori* sense what to assume for the physical nature of the stimulus."[418] Jackson went on to say, "I propose that, as the Shroud collapsed through the underlying body, radiation emitted from all points within that body discolored the cloth so as to produce the observed image."[419] As the radiation from the body began to interact with the fibrils of the cloth, the fibers on the surface were exposed to more radiation than the fibers within.[420]

As the Shroud dropped into the body region, different places on the cloth intersected the body surface at different times, "depending on how far that point was originally away from the body." Each part of the cloth received a dose of radiation "in proportion to the time that it [was] inside the emitting body region." Since the cloth on the dorsal side of the body did not move into the body the discoloration there was generated "only at point of contact" with the result that the dorsal image appeared "as a direct contact image."[421]

As the cloth fell into the body region, "internal stresses" within it caused it to "bulge away from the sides of the body and at the top of the head. Because the radiation was absorbed in the air, "very little dose [was] accumulated in the side and upper head regions of the cloth, and hence, no image [was] visible there."[422]

Jackson pointed out that electromagnetic radiation that is "absorbed strongly" in the air "consists of photons in the ultraviolet or soft x-ray region." These photons, "sufficiently energetic to photochemically modify cellulose" are "strongly absorbed in cellulose over fibril-like distances." Jackson's own experiments indicated that "subsequent aging in an oven of photosensitized (bleached) cloth by short-wave ultraviolet radiation produces a yellow-browned pattern like the Shroud body image," the result of "chemically altered cellulose."[423]

Therefore, Jackson argued, "radiation from the body initially photosensitized the body image onto the Shroud." If the radiation was ultraviolet, the pattern would have appeared as a bleached image on a darker cloth. "With time, natural aging would have reversed the relative shading of the image to its presently observed state where it appears darker than the surrounding cloth (which darkened with time, but not as fast)." This mechanism, he felt was consistent with: (1) "the observed lack of pyrolytic [pertaining to a chemical change caused by heat] products in microchemical studies of Shroud fibrils expected from high temperature cellulose degradation (in this case image coloring occurs by natural aging at ambient [surrounding] temperatures over a long period of time);" and (2) "the absence of substances in the image areas that chemically colored the cloth."[424]

As the Shroud was initially draped over a bloody body, Jackson was convinced, the blood was transferred by direct contact to the Shroud.[425] As the cloth collapsed into the body region, "each cloth point [fell] vertically downwards," so that "relative to the initial draping configuration of the Shroud over the body," the features of the image tended to "align vertically over their corresponding body part" — except where stresses in the cloth (mostly near the sides of the body images where the cloth flattened and bulged away from the body) interfered with the vertical motion.[426]

Jackson believed that the intensity of the image was determined solely by the time the cloth was in contact with the body region. If it was to be assumed that the "radiation event" operated "on a time scale less than the time for the upper part of the Shroud to fall completely through the body region" then "the interaction timed for cloth points, whether initially in contact with the frontal or dorsal surfaces of the body [were] equal," as were the image intensities at the initial contact points.[427]

The process Jackson proposed would explain the skeletal appearance of the fingers (which some other scientists explain as the result of blood loss). "If," he proposed, "the radiant emission varied with type of internal structure, such as tissue versus bone, then internal body structures might be convoluted into the general image picture." Although the surface details of the body of the man of the Shroud seem to dominate the image, because the "assumed volumetric emission of radiation" must have been "nearly homogeneous," the hand region "might be an example where an internal body structure dominated the image which normally recorded body surface topography." The long, bony appearance of the fingers might actually have been "images of the internal bones of the hand extending into the palm region, which, as the cloth passed through the handed region, recorded a greater dose than the surrounding tissue."[428]

According to Jackson's theory, when the upper part of the Shroud, the part that was pulled up and over the body to cover the face, chest, abdomen, and upper surfaces of the legs, fell into the body region, both sides of the cloth should have been irradiated. However, the radiation should have affected only the upper side of the dorsal image, because the part of the cloth on which the body rested stayed in place and never moved into the body. For this reason, Jackson hoped that a future examination of the Shroud would include removing the backing that was sewn onto the cloth after the 1532 fire. If this theory was true, the frontal image would be visible on both sides of the Shroud, while the dorsal image should appear on only one side.[429]

Jackson was convinced that his hypothesis of "a collapsing cloth into a radiating body" seemed to explain all the known characteristics of the Shroud image as well as suggest "certain testable predictions." The chief difficulty with his theory, he admitted, was to explain why a human body would behave in the manner he described. He was willing to admit that his "unconventional" theory required extensive studies and testing, but felt that the study of the Shroud of Turin, possibly "one of history's greatest scientific puzzles" might prove to represent "a valid case for rethinking certain concepts of modern science."[430]

The one thing that is certain about the Shroud is that, after a century of theories offered by various scientists and dozens of scientific tests, including radiocarbon-dating performed in the 1970s and 1980s, the origin of the image of the crucified man is as much a mystery as it was when the photographs taken by Secondo Pia in the 1890s strongly suggested that the cloth was not a garden-variety faked medieval relic.

Alan Adler noted that many researchers have tried to find "theoretical explanations" for the image. "John Jackson has come up with a couple. But not all of us buy what he thinks are some of the mechanisms because they seem to violate other physical laws." He went on to observe, "There are plenty of chemical processes that will produce the chemistry of the Shroud. There are plenty of processes that will produce the physics of the Shroud. What you have to do is find one that will produce the physics and the chemistry at the same time. . . . And if that's not bad enough, you have to also require that it produce the biological characteristics of the Shroud at the same time. And it's interesting that no matter what anyone has suggested, they haven't found a mechanism that will correctly explain the biological, physical, and chemical characteristics all at the same time"[431]

There are dozens of tests and procedures that scientists would have liked to perform on the Shroud, but none were planned, despite an exhibition in 1998 (and a scheduled exhibition in 2000). The major concern of nearly all those who have studied the artifact is its preservation. Ray Rogers expressed concern that the image will eventually fade away. This is because the image was caused by some phenomenon which caused certain parts of the fabric, in effect, to age prematurely. However, Rogers explained, "The rest of the cloth is continuing to age naturally. In relation to the background the image is getting dimmer and dimmer all the time. Some day the aging fabric is going to catch up with it and obliterate it."[432]

Conserving the Shroud with its image presents nearly as a great a problem as explaining the man of the Shroud. Alan Adler said in an interview, "People have seen things [on the cloth] that correspond to fungi, pollens . . . bacteria. . . . [W]e suggested they better [find out] . . . is there biological degradation? It's never been tested. And it's a serious problem in conservation. . . . [T]here is certainly fungi on the Shroud. And . . . you'd better find out what types and how much, because if you don't you're not going to be able to conserve it properly. . . . You'd better not talk about conserving it physically and chemically until you find out what's there. One of the things you'd like to do to conserve it, is put it under anaerobic conditions, so there's no longer any oxygen there, to oxidize the image physically or chemically. But you don't dare do that till you find out whether there are anaerobic [able to live without free oxygen] organisms there, who would now love to multiply and divide, and live on cellulose, since there's no oxygen there to keep them at a low level."[433]

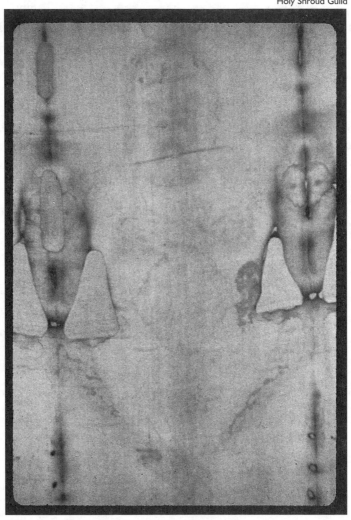

Photo from 1973 of the face and chest area.

Chapter XIII

'An Accurate Picture of the Passion'

Dozens of scientists and historians have devoted their attentions to the Shroud of Turin for a century, but it seems as if the mountains of data they have amassed have produced no definitive explanation concerning the origin of the remarkable image. It is easier to determine what the Shroud *is not* than what it *is*. It has been demonstrated *almost* beyond a doubt that the image is not a painting. Neither, it seems clear, is the image the impression of a statue. The body represented upon it is perfectly correct anatomically and the stains on the image that look like blood *are* indeed the blood of a real human being (or ape). It would seem that the image on the Shroud was almost certainly made by means of contact with a physically traumatized human body. No alternative explanation seems as plausible as this. Yet no one, working with any medium, has been able to devise a procedure capable of producing an image like that seen on the Shroud. Even when working with real cadavers, and even with twentieth-century technology, experimenters have not been able to create images that render the form of a crucified man that even approach the anatomical accuracy of the Shroud image.

Since carbon-dating performed on a portion of the cloth seems to indicate a medieval date, one is constrained to entertain the possibility that the image was created in the Middle Ages. Yet, when one considers the results of the various studies that have been made on the cloth, it is certainly much easier to believe that the Shroud preserves the image of a real man who was crowned with thorns, scourged, and crucified, than to believe it was the creation of an artist, or even the result of the special preparation of a cadaver. One would have to suppose the availability, at least six centuries ago, of technologies that must have surfaced and then disappeared totally unrecorded, that cannot be duplicated, even in the era of television, computers, and air and space travel. The various theories proposed to explain a medieval origin of the Shroud would, in the opinion of this writer, constitute almost as great a miracle as the Resurrection.

Even if one concedes that the Turin cloth in fact enshrouded a man who died in a manner identical to the way the writers of the Gospel describe the death of Jesus, this does not, however, *prove* that the image is in fact that of Jesus, much less that it came about by miraculous means. Alan Adler has said, "Just because we don't know [what caused the image] doesn't prove it's supernatural. It just means we don't know a process that can do this."[434]

Yves Delage, the French scientist who studied the Shroud in the early 1900s, believed that the image on the cloth was that of Jesus of Nazareth, even though he himself was an agnostic. He wrote in 1902, "A religious question has been unnecessarily introduced in a problem that is purely scientific, with the result that passions become heated and logic . . . derailed. If he had been, instead of Christ, a Sargon or an Achilles or a Pharaoh, nobody would have thought to raise any objections. . . . I accept Christ as a historical character and I do not understand that there could be anyone who would be scandalized if physical remains of His earthly life are still in existence."[435]

Adler, however, pointed out, "All the science in the world is never, ever going to prove the Shroud is authentic. . . . It's only capable of proving it's disauthentic. . . . There's no acceptable laboratory experiment for 'Christness.' We pointed that out to people four or five times in print, and nobody pays any attention."[436] John Heller declared that the Shroud's authenticity would not be proved, "Even if you had a signature on the lower right hand side, 'This is my Shroud, signed J. Christ. Attested to by the mayor of Jerusalem.' That's not scientific evidence. That's historical evidence."[437]

Only three of the members of STURP — John Jackson, Robert Bucklin, and Barry Schwortz — were willing to say that the Shroud was *probably* the actual burial sheet of Christ.[438] Nearly all the other members of the group, however, concluded that the cloth was not a fake or forgery, and that they found nothing to "disauthenticate" its identification with Jesus. Ray Rogers, when asked if the Shroud actually wrapped the body of Christ, spoke for the group when he said, "We do not have a test for Jesus Christ. So we can't hypothesize or test for that question."[439]

Yet another member of STURP, Don Lynn, made what might stand, until further extensive testing is accomplished, as the most cogent and reasonable explanation of the Shroud of Turin: "It is anatomically correct; it matches the Gospels historically; everything is correct with what we know. It is an accurate picture of the passion and death of Christ. It makes it very real that this was a man who was beaten and scourged and crucified. So the story is all there. Whether it is authentic or not is not important. What you have is the Gospel, the story of Christ crucified, set forth in detail before you, to look at, appreciate, and think about. Who made it is unimportant. So the final answer is not really that crucial, except as a challenging exercise."[440]

No study — not even the carbon-dating experiments of 1988 — has been able to demonstrate that the Shroud is *not* the authentic winding sheet that covered the body of Christ, while proof that it *is* such a relic is beyond the scope of science. Whether a relic or an icon, however, the Turin Shroud visually reveals with unimpeachable accuracy and in devastating detail, the sufferings of Jesus. This is a conclusion to which very few would object.

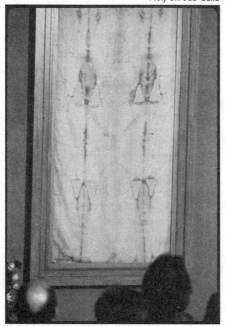

At left, a 1973 photo of the frontal image; below, another photo from 1973, this one of the wrist wound.

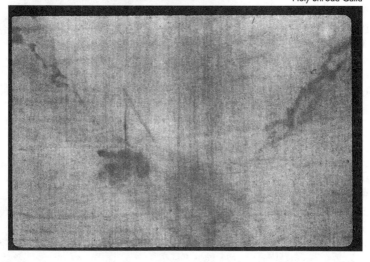

Medical
Illustrations

Palmer View of the Hand

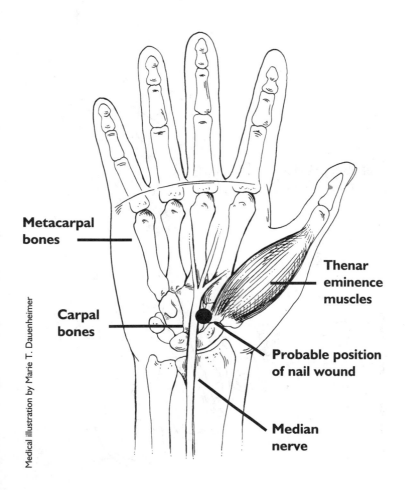

Metacarpal bones

Carpal bones

Thenar eminence muscles

Probable position of nail wound

Median nerve

Medical illustration by Marie T. Dauenheimer

Dorsal (Top) View of the Foot

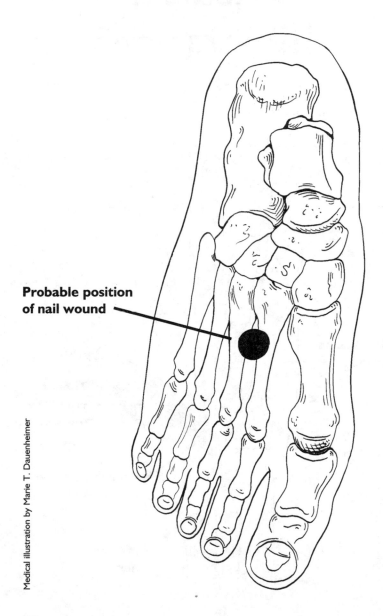

Probable position of nail wound

Medical illustration by Marie T. Dauenheimer

Anterior (Front) View

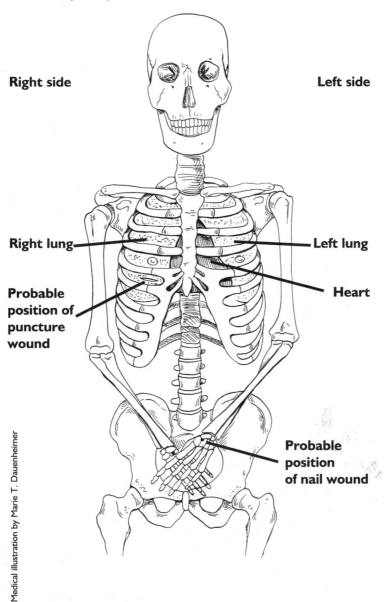

Right side

Left side

Right lung

Left lung

Probable
position of
puncture
wound

Heart

Probable
position
of nail wound

Medical illustration by Marie T. Dauenheimer

Notes

1. Ian Wilson, *The Mysterious Shroud.* (Garden City, NY: Doubleday, 1986), p. 181.
2. Orazio Petrosillo and Emanuela Marinelli, *The Enigma of the Shroud: Challenge to Science.* (Translated by Louis J. Scerri.) (San Gwann, Malta: Publishers Enterprises Group, 1996), p. 198.
3. Peter Rinaldi, *I Saw the Holy Shroud: A Study of the Shroud of Christ.* (New Rochelle, NY: Don Bosco Publications, n.d.), p.18.
4. *Ibid.* p. 19.
5. Petrosillo and Marinelli, *op. cit.* p. 166.
6. Petrosillo and Marinelli, *op. cit.* p. 213.
7. Rinaldi, *op. cit.* p. 46.
8. Frederick T. Zugibe, *The Cross and the Shroud.* (Cresskill, NJ: McDonagh & Co., 1981), p. 37.
9. William D. Edwards, Wesley J. Gabel, and Floyd E. Hosnier, "On the Physical Death of Jesus Christ," *The Journal of the American Medical Association,* Vol. 255, March 21, 1986, p. 1458.
10. *Ibid.*
11. Pierre Barbet, *A Doctor at Calvary.* (Translated by the Earl of Wicklow.) (Garden City, NY: Image Books, 1963), p. 39.
12. Edwards, et al., *op. cit.* p. 1459.
13. *Ibid.*
14. Petrosillo and Marinelli, *op. cit.* p. 228.
15. *Ibid.* p. 52.
16. Alexander Roberts and James Donaldson, *Ante-Nicene Fathers,* Vol. 4. (Peabody, MA: Hendrickson, 1995), p. 446.
17. William Meacham, "The Authentication of the Turin

Shroud: An Issue in Archaeological Epistemology," *Current Anthropology*, Vol. 24, no. 3 (June, 1983), p. 18.

18. Petrosillo and Marinelli, *op. cit.* p. 227.

19. Suetonius Tranquillus, *Lives of the Twelve Caesars.* (New York: Modern Library, 1931), p. 101.

20. N. Haas, "Anthropological Observations on the Skeletal Remains from Giv'at ha-Mivtar," *Israel Exploration Journal,* Vol. 20, 1970, pp. 38-59.

21. Rodney Hoare, *The Turin Shroud is Genuine: The Irrefutable Evidence.* (London: Souvenir Press, 1994), p. 68.

22. Reginald W. Rhein, "The Shroud of Turin: Medical Examiners Disagree," *Medical World News,* December 22, 1980, p. 50.

23. Peter Jennings, ed., *Face to Face with the Turin Shroud.* (Great Wakering, Essex, England: Mayhew-McCrimmon, 1978), p. 58.

24. Petrosillo and Marinelli, *op. cit.* p. 230-231.

25. *Ibid.* p. 165.

26. Zugibe, *op. cit.* p. 165.

27. *Ibid.* p. 160.

28. Robert Bucklin, "An Autopsy on the Man of the Shroud," a paper presented at the Third International Scientific Symposium on the Shroud of Turin, Nice, France, May 12, 1997, p. 2.

29. Jennings, *op. cit.* p. 57.

30. Rhein, *op. cit.* p. 50.

31. Giulio Ricci, "Historical, Medical, and Physical Study of the Holy Shroud," *Proceedings, 1977 US Conference of Research on the Shroud of Turin, March 23-24, Albuquerque, NM.* (Bronx, NY: Holy Shroud Guild, 1977), p. 61.

32. *Ibid.* p. 60-61.

33. *Ibid.* p. 60.

34. *Ibid.* p. 61.

35. Barbet, *op. cit.* p. 194.

36. Zugibe, *op. cit.* p. 19.

37. Bucklin, *op. cit.* p.6.

38. Barbet, *op. cit.* p. 95.
39. Mark Borkan, "Ecce Homo? Science and the Authenticity of the Turin Shroud," *Vertices, the Duke University Magazine of Science, Technology, and Medicine,* Winter 1995, Vol. X, no. 2, p. 26.
40. Wilson, *op. cit.* p. 20.
41. Barbet, *op. cit.* p. 95.
42. Wilson, *op. cit.* p. 20.
43. Jennings, *op. cit.* p. 58.
44. Bucklin, *op. cit.* p. 3.
45. Rhein, *op. cit.* p. 50.
46. *Ibid.*
47. Zugibe, *op. cit.* p. 33-35.
48. Rhein, *op. cit.* p. 50.
49. Borkan, *op. cit.* p. 26.
50. Bucklin, *op. cit.* p. 3.
51. Petrosillo and Marinelli, *op. cit.* p. 229.
52. Bucklin, *op. cit.* p. 3.
53. Jennings, *op. cit.* p. 58.
54. *Ibid.*
55. Wilson, *op. cit.* p. 34.
56. *Ibid.* pp. 4-5.
57. *Ibid.* p. 23.
58. Borkan, *op. cit.* p. 24.
59. *Ibid.* p. 25.
60. Jennings, *op. cit.* p. 58.
61. Zugibe, *op. cit.* p. 161.
62. Barbet, *op. cit.* pp. 109ff.
63. Zugibe, *op. cit.* p. 59.
64. Bucklin, *op. cit.* p. 5.
65. Zugibe, *op. cit.* p. 160.
66. Barbet, *op. cit.* p.119.
67. *Ibid.* p. 199.
68. Zugibe, *op. cit.* pp. 76-77.
69. *Ibid.*
70. Wilson, *op. cit.* p. 26.
71. Jennings, *op. cit.* p. 58.

72. Zugibe, *op. cit.* p. 65.

73. *Ibid.* pp. 25, 49.

74. Barbet, *op. cit.* p. 97.

75. Zugibe, *op. cit.* p. 143.

76. Bucklin, *op. cit.* p. 6.

77. Barbet, *op. cit.* pp. 97-98.

78. Bucklin, *op. cit.* p. 5.

79. Zugibe, *op. cit.* p. 163.

80. *Ibid.* p. 87.

81. *Ibid.* p. 27.

82. Rhein, *op. cit.* p. 50.

83. Wilson, *op. cit.* p. 26.

84. Wilson, *op. cit.* p. 34.

85. Bucklin, *op. cit.* pp. 3-4.

86. *Ibid.* p.7.

87. Zugibe, *op. cit.* pp. 162-163.

88. Wilson, *op. cit.* p. 129.

89. Jennings, *op. cit.* p. 59.

90. Borkan, *op. cit.* p. 26.

91. Rinaldi, *op. cit.* p. 68 .

92. Petrosillo and Marinelli, *op. cit.* pp. 230-231.

93. Bucklin, *op. cit.* pp. 8-9.

94. Barbet, *op. cit.* pp. 140-141.

95. *Ibid.* p. 108.

96. *Ibid.* pp. 201-202.

97. Zugibe, *op. cit.* pp. 94-95.

98. *Ibid.* pp. 135-136.

99. William D. Edwards, et al., *op. cit.* p. 1458.

100. Nickell, *op. cit.* p. 37.

101. Wilson, *op. cit.* pp. 45-46.

102. Ian Wilson, *The Blood and the Shroud: New Evidence that the World's Most Sacred Relic is Real.* (New York: Free Press, 1998), p. 55. (He cites a 1983 lecture by Victor Tunkel of Queen Mary College, University of London.)

103. Zugibe, *op. cit.* p. 152.

104. Ricci, *op. cit.* pp. 59-60.

105. Joseph A. Kohlbeck and Eugenia L. Nitowski, "New

Evidence May Explain Image on Shroud," *Biblical Archaeology Review,* July/August, 1986, p. 24.

106. Zugibe, *op. cit.* p. 233.

107. Borkan, *op. cit.* p. 36.

108. John A.T. Robinson, "The Shroud of Turin and the Grave-Clothes of the Gospel," *Proceedings, 1977 Conference of Research on the Shroud of Turin, March 23-24, 1977, Albuquerque, NM.* (Bronx, NY: Holy Shroud Guild, 1977), pp. 27-28.

109. *Ibid.*

110. *Ibid.*

111. *Ibid.* p. 28.

112. Alan D. Adler, "Updating Recent Studies on the Shroud of Turin," *Archaeological Chemistry: Organic, Inorganic, and Biochemical Analysis.* (Washington, DC: American Chemical Society, 1996), p. 226.

113. British Society for the Turin Shroud, issue #43, cited in "The Sudarium of Oviedo," http://www.shroud.com/bsts-4305.htm, pp. 1-2.

114. *Ibid.* p. 2.

115. *Ibid.*

116. Eusebius, *The History of the Christian Church.* (Translated by G.A. Williamso.) (Harmondsworth, England: Penguin, 1965), p. 100.

117. Philip Schaff and Henry Wace, *Nicene and Post-Nicene Fathers,* Vol. 3. (Peabody, MA: Hendrickson Publishers, 1995), p. 362.

118. Marjory Wardrop and J.O. Wardrop, "Life of St. Nino," *Studia Biblica et Ecclesiastica: Essays Chiefly in Biblical and Patristic Criticism by Members of the University of Oxford,* Vol. V, Part I. (Oxford: Clarendon Press, 1900), p. 72.

119. Charles Henry Lynch, ed., *Saint Braulio, Bishop of Saragossa (631-651), His Life and Writings.* (Washington: The Catholic University of America, 1938), pp. 96-97.

120. Scavone, *op. cit.* p. 76.

121. Thomas Wright, ed., *Early Travels in Palestine.* (New York: KTAV Publishing House, 1968), pp. 1-12.

122. Eusebius, *op. cit.* p. 67.

123. Scavone, *op. cit.* p. 81.

124. Alexander Roberts and James Donaldson, eds., *The Ante-Nicene Fathers,* Vol. 8. (Peabody, MA: Hendrickson Publishers, 1995), p. 558.

125. Evagrius Scholastic, *A History of the Church in Six Books, from A.D. 431 to A.D. 594.* (London: Samuel Bagster, 1846), pp. 219-221.

126. Scavone, *op. cit.* p. 76.

127. *Ibid.* p. 88.

128. Borkan, *op. cit.* p. 35.

129. Ian Wilson, *Holy Faces, Secret Places: An Amazing Quest for the Face of Jesus.* (New York: Doubleday, 1991), p. 141.

130. Scavone, *op. cit.* p. 82.

131. Wilson, *Mysterious Shroud,* p. 120.

132. Scavone, *op. cit.* p. 83.

133. Arnold Toynbee, *Constantine Porphyrogenitus and His Times.* (London: Oxford University Press, 1973), p. 186.

134. Scavone, *op. cit.* p. 86.

135. *The Catholic World Report*, April, 1993, p. 49.

136. Wilson, *Holy Faces*, p. 153.

137. Petrosillo and Marinelli, *op. cit.* p. 178.

138. *Ibid.*

139. John Heller, *Report on the Shroud of Turin.* (Boston: Houghton-Mifflin, 1983), p. 73.

140. Petrosillo and Marinelli, *op. cit.* p. 178.

141. Roland H. Bainton, *Here I Stand: A Life of Martin Luther.* (Nashville: Abingdon Press, 1950), p. 71.

142. Petrosillo and Marinelli, *op. cit.* p. 296.

143. *Ibid.* p. 179.

144. Wilson, *Holy Faces,* p. 154.

145. Wilson, *The Blood and the Shroud,* pp. 146-147.

146. Heller, *op. cit.* pp. 69-70.

147. *Ibid.* p. 70.

148. *Ibid.* p. 71.

149. *Ibid.* p. 72.

Notes

150. Petrosillo and Marinelli, p. 179.
151. *Ibid.* p. 180.
152. Wilson, *Mysterious Shroud,* p. 117.
153. Scavone, *op. cit.* p. 96.
154. *Ibid.* pp. 96-97.
155. *Ibid.* p. 97.
156. Vignon, Paul, *The Shroud of Christ.* (New Hyde Park, NY: University Books, 1970), pp. 67-68.
157. Richard W. Kaeuper and Elspeth Kennedy, *The Book of Chivalry of Geoffroi de Charny.* (Philadelphia: University of Pennsylvania Press, 1996), p. 3.
158. *Ibid.* p. 149.
159. *Ibid.* p. 151.
160. *Ibid.* p. 161.
161. *Ibid.* p. 197.
162. Ian Wilson, "Highlights of the Undisputed History," 1996, http:/www/shroud.com/history.htm, p. 2.
163. Wilson, *Mysterious Shroud,* p. 11.
164. Heller, *op. cit.* p. 17.
165. Nickell, *op. cit.* p. 12.
166. Wilson, *Mysterious Shroud,* p. 11.
167. Petrosillo and Marinelli, *op. cit.* p. 182.
168. Nickell, *op. cit.* p. 17.
169. Wilson, "Highlights of the Undisputed History," pp. 3-4.
170. *Ibid.* p. 4.
171. *Ibid.*
172. *Ibid.*
173. Wilson, "Highlights of the Undisputed History," p. 5.
174. Herbert Thurston, "The Holy Shroud," *The Catholic Encyclopedia*, Vol. XIII. (New York: Robert Appleton, 1913), p. 762.
175. Nickell, *op. cit.* p. 27.
176. Wilson, "Highlights of the Undisputed History," p. 8.
177. Jennings, *op. cit.* p. 26.
178. *Ibid.* p. 27.
179. Thurston, *op. cit.* p. 763.
180. *Ibid.*

181. Rinaldi, *op. cit.* p. 81.
182. Walter McCrone, *Judgment Day for the Turin Shroud.* (Chicago: Microscope Publications, 1996), pp. 3-4.
183. Borkan, *op. cit.* p. 21.
184. *Ibid.*
185. *Ibid.*
186. Scavone, *op. cit.* p. 30.
187. Alan D. Adler, telephone interview, August 15, 1997.
188. McCrone, *Judgment Day,* p. 17.
189. *Ibid.* p. 219.
190. *Ibid.* pp. 19-20.
191. Borkan, *op. cit.* p. 21.
192. Petrosillo and Marinelli, *op. cit.* p. 203.
193. Ibid. p. 202.
194. Paul Maloney, "The Current Status of Pollen Research and Prospects for the Future," *The ASSIST Newsletter*, June, 1990, Vol. 2, no. p. 8.
195. Petrosillo and Marinelli, *op. cit.* p. 204.
196. *Ibid.* p. 205.
197. Alan D. Adler, telephone interview, August 15, 1997.
198. Maloney, *op. cit.* p. 6.
199. *Ibid.*
200. Petrosillo and Marinelli, *op. cit.* p. 205.
201. Scavone, *op. cit.* p. 35.
202. *Ibid.* p. 39.
203. *Ibid.* p. 40.
204. Borkan, *op. cit.* p. 22.
205. Heller, *op. cit.* p. 64.
206. Petrosillo and Marinelli, *op. cit.* p. 27.
207. Rinaldi, *op. cit.* p. 82.
208. Heller, *op. cit.* p. 118.
209. *Ibid.* p. 55.
210. Alan D. Adler, telephone interview, August 15, 1997.
211. Heller, *op. cit.* p. 56.
212. Wilson, *Mysterious Shroud,* p. 54.
213. Heller, *op. cit.* pp. 115-116.
214. *Ibid.* p. 117.

215. Borkan, *op. cit.* p. 22.
216. *Ibid.* pp. 40-41.
217. *Ibid.* pp. 41-42.
218. Scavone, *op. cit.* p. 47.
219. *Ibid.* p. 48.
220. *Ibid.* p. 51.
221. *Ibid.* p. 52.
222. *Ibid.*
223. Thomas W. Case, *The Shroud of Turin and the C-14 Dating Fiasco: A Scientific Detective Story.* (Cincinnati: White Horse Press, 1996), p. 55.
224. Scavone, *op. cit.* p. 53.
225. Borkan, *op. cit.* p. 23.
226. Heller, *op. cit.* p. 216.
227. *Ibid.* pp. 216-217.
228. Case, *op. cit.* p. 13.
229. Scavone, *op. cit.* p. 54.
230. *Ibid.* p. 55.
231. Nickell, *op. cit.* p. 135.
232. Walter C. McCrone, "Microscopical Study of the Turin 'Shroud,' IV," *The Microscope.* (Chicago: McCrone Research Institute, ca. 1986), p. 84.
233. *Ibid.* p. 77.
234. Scavone, *op. cit.* p. 57.
235. McCrone, *op. cit.* p. 77.
236. *Ibid.*
237. *Ibid.* p. 85.
238. *Ibid.* pp. 91-92.
239. Scavone, *op. cit.* p. 57.
240. *Ibid.* p. 58.
241. Wilson, *Mysterious Shroud,* p. 89.
242. Heller, *op. cit.* pp. 139-140.
243. *Ibid.* p. 154.
244. *Ibid.* p. 140.
245. McCrone, *op. cit.* p. 77.
246. *Ibid.* pp. 92-93.
247. Robert A. Wild, "The Shroud of Turin: Probably the Work

of a 14th Century Forger," *Biblical Archaeology Review,* Vol. IX, no. 2, March/April 1984, p. 38.

248. McCrone, *Judgment Day,* p. 306.
249. *Ibid.* p. 322.
250. *Ibid.* pp. 302-303.
251. *Ibid.* p. 325; I know from personal experience that Father Peter believed that the Shroud was authentic. After meeting him for the first time, I wrote in my diary on July 27, 1990: "Fr. Rinaldi, who is 80, was very warm and friendly. He talked about his researches and his belief in the miraculous nature of the Shroud. [The members of STURP] all believe that the Radio Carbon-dating was done in an invalid way. He is searching for the opportunity to have new tests done. He seems to believe very strongly in the authenticity of the Shroud."
252. *Ibid.* p. 289.
253. Case, *op. cit.* p. 51.
254. Heller, *op. cit.* p. 1.
255. *Ibid.* p. 167.
256. *Ibid.* p. 133.
257. *Ibid.* p. 178.
258. *Ibid.* p. 180.
259. *Ibid.* p. 113.
260. Scavone, *op. cit.* p. 60.
261. *Ibid.* p. 61.
262. Case, *op. cit.* p. 53.
263. Case, *op. cit.* p. 53.
264. Heller, *op. cit.* p. 152.
265. Scavone, *op. cit.* p. 60.
266. Heller, *op. cit.* p. 209.
267. *Ibid.* pp. 208-211.
268. *Ibid.* p. 210
269. Heller, *op. cit.* p. 213.
270. *Ibid.* pp. 215-216.
271. Case, *op. cit.* p. 56.
272. *Ibid.* pp. 57-58.
273. Wilson, *The Blood and the Shroud,* p. 82.

274. *Ibid.* p. 39.
275. Gilbert R. Lavoie, *Unlocking the Secrets of the Shroud.* (Allen, TX: Thomas More, 1998), p. 86.
276. *Ibid. p.* 111.
277. Wilson, *The Blood and the Shroud,* p. 91.
278. *Ibid.* p. 90.
279. Kohlbeck and Nitowski, *op. cit.* pp. 23-24.
280. Robert Bucklin, "Autopsy on the Man of the Shroud," a paper delivered at the Third International Scientific Symposium on the Shroud of Turin, Nice, France, 12 May 1997, p. 3.
281. Borkan, *op. cit.* p. 28.
282. Alan D. Whanger, "A Reply to Doubts Concerning the Coins Over the Eyes," *The Holy Shroud Guild Newsletter,* Vol. 3, 1997, no. 56, December, 1997, p. 7.
283. Ricci, *op. cit.* pp. 89-90.
284. "Research by Dr. and Mrs. Whanger," Council for the Study of the Shroud of Turin, http://dmi-www.mc. duke.edu/shroud/whanger.htm.
285. Borkan, *op. cit.* p. 28.
286. *Ibid*, pp. 28-29.
287. Wilson, *Mysterious Shroud*, p. 133.
288. Alan D. Whanger, "A Reply to Doubts. . .", p. 7.
289. Mario Moroni, "Pontius Pilate's Coin on the Right Eye of the Man in the Holy Shroud in the Light of New Archaeo-logical Findings," *Symposium Proceedings: History, Science, Theology, and the Shroud,* St. Louis, MO, USA, June 22-23, 1991. (Amarillo, TX: The Man in the Shroud Committee of Amarillo, 1991), p. 293.
290. *Ibid.* p. 278.
291. Borkan, *op. cit.* p. 28.
292. Dr. Alan and Mrs. Mary Whanger, "Floral, Coin, and Other Non-Body Images on the Shroud of Turin: A Summary," *The Assist Newsletter,* December, 1989, pp. 1-3.
293. "Research by Dr. and Mrs. Whanger," Council for Study of the Shroud of Turin, http://dmi-www.mc.duke.edu/shroud/whanger.htm.

294. Borkan, *op. cit.* p. 29.

295. Wilson, *Mysterious Shroud*, p. 110.

296. Petrosillo and Marinelli, *op. cit.* p. 192.

297. Wilson, *Mysterious Shroud*, p. 107.

298. *Ibid.* p. 110.

299. Borkan, *op. cit.* p. 34.

300. Petrosillo and Marinelli, *op. cit.* p. 196.

301. Wilson, *Holy Faces,* pp. 173-174.

302. Borkan, *op. cit.* p. 38.

303. *Ibid.* p. 37.

304. Petrosillo and Marinelli, *op. cit.* p. 142.

305. Case, *op. cit.* pp. 76-77.

306. Borkan, *op. cit.* p. 39.

307. *Ibid.*

308. Petrosillo and Marinelli, *op. cit.* p. 55.

309. Borkan, *op. cit.* p. 39.

310. Alan Adler, telephone interview, August 15, 1997.

311. Petrosillo and Marinelli, *op. cit.* p. 80.

312. *Ibid.* p. 92.

313. *Ibid.* p. 97.

314. *Ibid.* pp. 97-98.

315. *Holy Shroud Guild Newsletter,* November, 1988, pp. 3-4.

316. Petrosillo and Marinelli, *op. cit.* p. 12.

317. *Ibid.*

318. Remarks at Holy Shroud Seminar Retreat, Mount Esopus, NY, August 24, 1996, and telephone interview with Alan Adler, August 15, 1997.

319. Petrosillo and Marinelli, *op. cit.* p. 117.

320. *Ibid.* p. 102.

321. *Ibid.* p. 104.

322. *Ibid.* p. 243.

323. *Ibid. p.* 109.

324. *Holy Shroud Guild Newsletter,* March 30, 1995, p. 3.

325. Borkan, *op. cit.* p. 39.

326. *Ibid.* p. 4.

327. Case, *op. cit.* pp. 77-78.

328. *Ibid.* pp. 78-79.

Notes

329. *Holy Shroud Guild Newsletter,* September, 1989, p. 4.
330. Petrosillo and Marinelli, *op. cit.* p. 147.
331. Borkan, *op. cit.* p. 38.
332. "The Carbon Date for the Shroud of Turin," *The ASSIST Newsletter,* Vol. 1, no. 1, n.d., p. 7.
333. "The Carbon Date for the Shroud," *ASSIST,* p. 7.
334. *Holy Shroud Guild Newsletter,* September, 1989, p. 4.
335. Case, *op. cit.,* pp. 82, 85.
336. Borkan, *op. cit.* p. 40.
337. *Holy Shroud Guild Newsletter,* May 15, 1991, p. 4.
338. "The Carbon Date for the Shroud," *ASSIST,* pp. 1, 7-8.
339. *Ibid.* p. 8.
340. Petrosillo and Marinelli, *op. cit.* pp. 248-249.
341. *Holy Shroud Guild Newsletter,* November 25, 1995, p. 2.
342. Petrosillo and Marinelli, *op. cit.* p. 249.
343. Case, *op. cit.* pp. 37-38.
344. Wilson, *The Blood and the Shroud*, p. 221.
345 *Ibid.* p. 38.
346. John P. Jackson, telephone interview, August 21, 1997.
347. Harry E. Gove, *Relic, Icon, or Hoax? Carbon Dating the Turin Shroud.* (Bristol: Institute of Physics Publishing, 1996), p. 308.
348. Wilson, *The Blood and the Shroud*, p. 227.
349. *Ibid.*
350. Wilson, *The Blood and the Shroud,* p. 224.
351. John P. Jackson, telephone interview, August 21, 1997.
352. Alan D. Adler, telephone interview, August 15, 1997.
353. Alan D. Adler, "Updating Recent Studies on the Shroud of Turin," *Archaeological Chemistry: Organic, Inorganic, and Biochemical Agents.* n.p., American Chemical Society, 1996, p. 325.
354. *Ibid.,* p. 226.
355. Nickell, *op. cit.* p. 55
356. Lynn Pincknett and Clive Prince, *Turin Shroud: In Whose Image? The Truth Behind the Centuries-Long Conspiracy of Silence.* (New York: Harper Collins, 1994), p. 139.
357. Gove, *op. cit.* p. 290.

358. *Holy Shroud Guild Newsletter,* March 15, 1992.
359. *Ibid.* September 20, 1990,
360. Rinaldi, *op. cit.* p. 72.
361. John P. Jackson, "An Unconventional Hypothesis to Explain all Image Characteristics Found on the Shroud Image," *Symposium Proceedings: History, Science, Theology, and the Shroud*, St. Louis, MO, USA, June 22-23, 1991. (Amarillo, TX: The Man in the Shroud Committee, 1991), pp. 325-328.
362. Wild, *op. cit.* p. 46.
363. Gove, *op. cit.* p. 297.
364. Nickell, *op. cit.* p. 106.
365. Wilson, *Mysterious Shroud*, p. 66.
366. Borkan, *op. cit.* pp. 40-41.
367. Wilson, *The Blood and the Shroud,* pp. 202-203.
368. *Borkan, op. cit.* p. 44.
369. Isabel Piczek, "Is the Turin Shroud a Painting?" *Symposium Proceedings: History, Science, Theology, and the Shroud*. St. Louis, MO, USA, June 22-23, 1991. (Amarillo, TX: The Man in the Shroud Committee, 1991), p. 271.
370. Borkan, *op. cit.* p. 44.
371. *Ibid.* p. 45; in Wilson, *The Blood and the Shroud,* an instance is mentioned in which a man who died in a nursing home in Liverpool, England, in 1981, left "an indelible imprint" of a hand, his buttocks, shoulders, and jaws on the mattress on which he died. But these features appear only as "simple outlines and blocks of shadows" and there is nothing unusual about the negatives of these impressions. Apparently no one has been able to account for this phenomenon (p. 209).
372. Petrosillo and Marinelli, *op. cit.* p. 212.
373. *Ibid.*
374. Wilson, *Mysterious Shroud,* pp. 68-69.
375. Pincknett and Prince, *op. cit.* p. 175.
376. *Ibid.* p. 178.
377. *Ibid.* pp. 157-159.
378. *Ibid.* p. 183.

379. *Ibid.* p. 179.
380. *Ibid.* p. 185.
381. *Ibid.* p. 184.
382. *Ibid.* p. 185.
383. Isabel Piczek, "Alice in Wonderland and the Shroud of Turin?" an address given at the Holy Shroud Seminar Retreat at Mount Esopus, New York, August 24, 1996, pp. 8-9.
384. Christopher Knight and Robert Lomas, *The Second Messiah: Templars, The Turin Shroud, and the Great Secret of Freemasonry.* (London: Century Books, 1997), p. 147.
385. Wilson, *The Blood and the Shroud*, pp. 213-215.
386. *Ibid.* p. 217.
387. *Ibid.* p. 60.
388. Piczek, "Alice in Wonderland," pp. 13-14.
389. Knight and Lomas, *op. cit.* p. 77.
390. *Ibid.* p. 79.
391. *Ibid.* p. 87.
392. *Ibid.* pp. 168-169.
393. *Ibid.* pp. 195-196.
394. Paul Vignon, *The Shroud of Christ.* (New Hyde Park, NY: University Books, 1970), p. 169.
395. Borkan, *op. cit.* p. 41.
396. Petrosillo and Marinelli, *op. cit.* pp. 219-220.
397. Rinaldi, *op. cit.* p. 64.
398. *Ibid.* p. 221.
399. Kohlbeck and Nitowski, *op. cit.* pp. 26-28.
400. Petrosillo and Marinelli, *op. cit.* p. 221.
401. Nickell, *op. cit.* p. 87.
402. *Los Alamos Monitor,* March 24, 1978.
403. Petrosillo and Marinelli, *op. cit.* p. 221.
404. *Holy Shroud Guild Newsletter*, March 30, 1990, p. 4.
405. *ASSIST Newsletter*, vol. 1, no. 1, p. 7.
406. *Holy Shroud Guild Newsletter*, March 30, 1990, p. 4.
407. Case, *op. cit.* p. 89.
408. *Ibid.* p. 90.
409. Borkan, *op. cit.* p. 42.

410. *Ibid.* pp. 42-43.
411. Petrosillo and Marinelli, *op. cit.* p. 222.
412. *Ibid.*
413. John P. Jackson, "An Unconventional Hypothesis," p. 332.
414. *Ibid.* p. 333.
415. *Ibid.* p. 335.
416. *Ibid.* pp. 336-337.
417. *Ibid.* p. 339.
418. *Ibid.*
419. *Ibid.*
420. *Ibid.* p. 340.
421. *Ibid.* pp. 340-341.
422. *Ibid.* p. 341.
423. *Ibid.*
424. *Ibid.*
425. *Ibid.*
426. *Ibid.* pp. 341-342.
427. *Ibid.* p. 342.
428. *Ibid.*
429. *Ibid.* p. 343.
430. *Ibid.* pp. 343-344.
431. Case, *op. cit.* p. 70.
432. Borkan, *op. cit.* p. 43.
433. Case, *op. cit.* pp. 90-92.
434. *Ibid.* p. 70.
435. Petrosillo and Marinelli, *op. cit.* p. 997.
436. Case, *op. cit.* p. 94.
437. *Ibid.* pp. 94-95.
438. Heller, *op. cit.* p. 220.
439. *Ibid.* pp. 216-217.
440. *Ibid.* p. 220.

Index

Index

Our Sunday Visitor...
Your Source for Discovering the Riches of the Catholic Faith

Our Sunday Visitor has an extensive line of materials for young children, teens, and adults. Our books, Bibles, booklets, CD-ROMs, audios, and videos are available in bookstores worldwide.

To receive a FREE full-line catalog or for more information, call **Our Sunday Visitor** at **1-800-348-2440**. Or write, **Our Sunday Visitor** / 200 Noll Plaza / Huntington, IN 46750.

Please send me: __ A catalog
Please send me materials on:
   __ Apologetics and catechetics   __ Reference works
   __ Prayer books   __ Heritage and the saints
   __ The family   __ The parish

Name_____

Address_____Apt._____

City_____State___Zip_____

Telephone ( )_____

                                            A93BBABP

Please send a friend: __ A catalog
Please send a friend materials on:
   __ Apologetics and catechetics   __ Reference works
   __ Prayer books   __ Heritage and the saints
   __ The family   __ The parish

Name_____

Address_____Apt._____

City_____State___Zip_____

Telephone ( )_____

                                            A93BBABP

 Our Sunday Visitor
200 Noll Plaza
Huntington, IN 46750
1-800-348-2440
osvbooks@osv.com

Your Source for Discovering the Riches of the Catholic Faith